MILESTONES OF THOUGHT

St. John of the Cross

THE DARK NIGHT
OF THE SOUL

Translated, abridged, and edited
by
KURT F. REINHARDT
Stanford University

D1114415

FREDERICK UNGAR PUBLISHING CO.
NEW YORK

MILESTONES
OF THOUGHT
in the History of Ideas

Nihil obstat
Benedictus M. Blank, O.P. M.S.T.
Censor deputatus

Imprimi licet
John J. Mitty
Archiepiscopus Sti. Francisci in California

Third Printing

Copyright 1957 by
Frederick Ungar Publishing Co.

Printed in the United States of America

Library of Congress Catalog Card Number: 56-12399

INTRODUCTION

ST. JOHN OF THE CROSS AND
CHRISTIAN MYSTICISM

St. John of the Cross (1542-1591) is generally regarded as one of the greatest—if not the greatest—of Christian mystics. This high estimate of his life and work received official sanction when, on July 27, 1926, Pope Pius XI by solemn declaration raised the Spanish scholar and poet to the dignity of a "Doctor of the Church." In order that the reader may better understand the doctrine set forth in the two major works presented here in a new translation and in an abridged version, it is necessary to give a brief exposition of the nature of mysticism in general and of Christian mysticism in particular.

I. Christian Mysticism

In the history and the comparative psychology of religion as well as in popular usage the word "mysticism" occurs in various shades of meaning, ranging all the way from the crudest connotations to the most sublime. The term is at times applied almost indiscriminately to certain orgiastic states of mind produced by intoxicants or other artificial stimuli, to hysterical and other psychopathic states, to the phenomena of occultism and spiritism, as well as to spiritual experiences which relate to the itinerary of the soul to God.

To test and evaluate the claims of the several kinds of "mysticism" that we meet with in the course of the centuries in Orient and Occident, the safest way to escape confusion and idle speculation seems to be to turn to the testimony of those who might be called the practitioners of the mystical life, that is, the mystics themselves.

Weighing the variegated documents of mystical experience, one arrives at something that may be called the common property of all mysticism. This common denominator is suggested by the original meaning of the word. The Greek verb *myein* means to close, to veil, to cover over, and the Greek noun *mysterion* denotes a secret or a mystery. Mysticism in a most general sense, then, signifies self-communion, meditation, and contemplation in quietude. This implies further a return from manifoldness and dispersion to unity and simplicity.

Now this general and common characteristic of all mystical theory and practice almost coincides with the root-meaning of the word *religion*. The Latin noun *religio* derives from the verb *re-ligere* or *re-legere,* that is, to re-unite, to bring back, to bind together. "Religion" thus marks the end of some state of disharmony, of alienation or estrangement, and denotes homecoming, reconciliation, and peace.

Generally speaking, then, the ways of both mysticism and religion lead from the external to the internal, from distraction to recollection and union. Within this general frame, however, several layers or strata may be distinguished. We may use the term *natural* or *cosmic mysticism* to designate specific empirical elements that are present in all mystical experience but which, in the case of *Christian* or *biblical mysticism,* form only the sub-stratum of the supernatural and purely spiritual "superstructure."

It would seem furthermore that even the most general description and definition of mysticism must take account of the reality of the spiritual human soul, a spiritual reality that was not superadded subsequent to the advent of Christ and Christianity, but which must be conceived as an aboriginal quality of the human soul. This is the reason why, according to the teaching of Christian theology and philosophy, even in the soul of a pagan (such as Plato or Plotinus) there may be found an adequate disposition for a knowledge of God, corresponding to the natural activity of God within the spiritual soul.

There is, however, one essential difference between any merely natural or cosmic mysticism and supernatural or Christian-biblical mysticism: while natural mysticism does not recognize or is apt to forget the all-important qualitative distinction between nature and supernature, immanence and transcendence, the soul and God, Christian mysticism insists not only that the personal Creator-God is both immanent and transcendent, both within the world and the soul and above them, but also that the world and God, creature and Creator, the finite and the infinite are actually incommensurable. While cosmic mysticism thus easily succumbs to the temptation of pantheistically proclaiming the identity of the world and God (cf. Spinoza's *Deus sive natura*), Christian mysticism sees man separated from God by an abyss which cannot be bridged over by any human effort, but only by the initiative of God Himself. By the infusion of grace, God may illumine and elevate the human soul, and in this descending movement of love (*agape*) He may meet the ascending loving aspiration of the soul (*eros*). Again, while both oriental and occidental cosmic mysticism are inclined to regard *personality* as a limitation and an impediment on the way to mystical union, Christian mysticism sees in personality a crowning perfection, although it strongly affirms the real and absolute distinction between the finite personality of man and the infinite personality of God. The personal God of the biblical religion is immanent in the world and in the soul by His essence (*per essentiam*), and transcendent as the "totally Other," Who infinitely surpasses that world of creatures which He yet sustains in its being by His substantial omnipresence.

According to traditional Christian theology and philosophy, the human soul is a *forma sui generis* (i.e., an independent substance) and as such capable of existing and acting in a twofold manner: (1) in union with the body and its activities; (2) independently, as a pure spirit, in accordance with its spiritual nature. As far as natural mysticism is concerned, the experimental knowledge of God (*cognitio ex-*

perimentalis Dei), of which the mystics speak, denotes an awareness of the natural activity of God within the soul, by means of introspection and meditation. This kind of experience is minutely described in the *Enneads* of Plotinus (203-269). No extraordinary grace is needed for this type of religious experience. The spiritual soul here becomes conscious of its divine origin; it feels itself separated from and yet part of the plenitude of Divine Being, and it is longing with an ardent desire (*eros*) for reunion and communion with the absolute ground in which it originated.

Some Greek as well as some Hindu philosophers (e.g., Sankara) were familiar with the "three ways" of mystical experience: the way of purgation or purification, the way of illumination, and the way of unity or union. Both Christian and non-Christian mysticism developed a variable and sometimes complex scale of "steps" of meditation and contemplation which all in the last analysis may be reduced to the basic "three ways."

On the first and second way the soul is *actively* engaged in preparing itself by discursive reasoning and meditation for the third way of "mystical union." These preparatory steps are usually said to pertain to *asceticism* (from Greek *askein:* to train, to exercise) rather than to *mysticism* in the strict sense. The way of *purification* consists essentially in the liberation of the soul from sensory apprehensions and images. The way of *illumination* is to make the thus liberated soul capable of practising the *cardinal virtues* of prudence, justice, temperance, and fortitude and (with the aid of infused sanctifying grace) the *theological* (or strictly supernatural) *virtues* of faith, hope, and love (*caritas*).

Concerning these preliminary steps, Plotinus writes: "Let him who is able to do so commune with himself, but let him leave aside what the glance of the eye beholds. Let him not look backward to those things which formerly blinded his eyes with the splendor of bodily beauty. . . . Retreat into yourself and look at yourself, and if you behold yourself as not yet beautiful, then act as the sculptor does:

chip away from your self all superfluous things, and never cease working on your own image, until the splendor of divine virtues is beginning to bathe you in its light. Only the purified eye beholds the plenitude of beauty. But if it tries to see while darkened by vice, while impure or weak, it cannot endure this radiant brightness and sees nothing. The eye that wants to see must be assimilated to the object that is to be seen. Never indeed would the eye behold the sun unless there were something sun-like in the eye itself." After reading the *Enneads,* Goethe poetically expressed the identical idea in the famous lines:

> Wär' nicht das Auge sonnenhaft,
> Die Sonne könnt' es nie erblicken;
> Wär' nicht in uns des Gottes eigne Kraft,
> Wie könnt' uns Göttliches entzücken?

Psychologists and psychiatrists have pointed out certain parallels which seemingly exist between mystical experiences and pathological (especially hysterical and neurotic) states of mind. Although it can hardly be denied that superficially such parallels occasionally do exist, there is this important difference: while the exaltation, the mental and emotional strain, and the patterns of simplification in thinking and doing that are observed in connection with several forms of mental disease are in all instances followed by distraction, exhaustion, and a general impoverishment of the mind, the genuine mystical experience brings in its wake effects of a totally different kind: a simplicity of mind that derives from a rich and deeply recollected mental activity, and a heightened intensity of purpose and resolve. William James, in his significant work on "The Varieties of Religious Experience," has nothing but scorn for the endeavors of some psychologists who are trying to circumvent inconvenient facts in psychological and psychiatric research by applying to them psychopathological labels.

Generally speaking, the integrity and genuineness of

mystical experience must be doubted whenever the mystical phenomena are produced artificially, either by psycho-technical devices or by a convulsive overexertion of the mental and emotional faculties. In these instances the experience is often accompanied by vague and at times hallucinatory imaginings and by a greatly increased egocentricity; and it is usually followed by nervous exhaustion and by morbid anxiety and disquietude. In short, the individual in this case becomes more and more unfit to perform the ordinary tasks and obligations of daily life. The genuine mystical experience, on the other hand, tends to harmonize and concentrate the faculties and activities, and this results in strengthened energy and vitality, in a healthy spiritual and social reorientation and, consequently, in a greater aptitude for the fulfillment of the demands of individual and social life.

Some renowned authors of the past and present (Luther, Pascal, Kierkegaard, Karl Barth, among others) have asserted that there is an intrinsic contradiction and opposition between rational philosophy, on the one hand, and theology (especially mystical theology), on the other; between "the God of reason" and "the God of faith," between "the God of philosophers" and "the God of Abraham, Isaac, and Jacob." In particular it has been claimed that Christian *mysticism* is opposed to medieval and modern *scholasticism,* especially in its Thomistic form. This contention is most easily disposed of by pointing to the fact that many of the outstanding scholastic thinkers, such as St. Albert the Great, St. Thomas Aquinas, St. Bonaventure, John Gerson, and others, were at the same time eminent mystics and the authors of works on mystical theology.

It is one of the great achievements of St. Thomas Aquinas (in whose footsteps St. John of the Cross follows in this as in many other respects) to have validated the power of human reason and therewith the independence of philosophy as a rational discipline in its own particular sphere. St. Thomas thus avoided the twin fallacies of rationalism and fideism. He demonstrated both the validity and the limits of reason in its attempt to attain to a knowledge of God. He agreed with Dionysius the Areopagite that finite human reason can never rise to an adequate or immediate knowledge of the Divine Essence, and that in this sense therefore the Deity remains for the philosopher an "unknown God." In the words of Etienne Gilson, "We know *that* He is, and we also know what He is not; but *what* He is remains wholly unknown." Or, in the words of St. Gregory of Nyssa, "Reason understands that the true knowledge and vision of that God for Whom it searches consist in seeing that He is invisible and in knowing that He transcends all knowledge."

This means then that the Divine Nature or Essence cannot be comprehended by human reason, not because this Essence is "irrational," but because it is "supra-rational" or strictly above the natural light of reason. But where reason fails, *faith* succeeds. And faith, which is a limited participation in the knowledge with which God knows Himself, penetrates into the dark light of the Divine mystery and learns to know God not only as the One Who is All, but as the One Who is both within all and above all. And it is in the "mysteries of faith" that Christian mysticism has its roots and its habitat. Christian mysticism is the fruit of Christian faith and revelation, and Christian theology finds its fulfillment in that *mystical theology* which is "the living encounter with the living God (J. Daniélou).

Philosophy is for the Christian theologian and mystic, in the words of Heidegger, "only a preliminary tool." It compels reason to acknowledge the *existence* of God, but it is incapable of comprehending His *essence*. It is ultimately led to a point where it must call itself in question by acknowledging and affirming the necessity and actuality of a wholly suprarational faith and revelation.

Christian revelation is an appeal of God addressed to man to partake of the life of Christ with the aid of the gifts of the Holy Spirit. According to Jan van Ruysbroek (1294-1381), the great Dutch mystic, the Divine life, "though it abides forever in the Father, flows forth with the Son, and

flows back again with the Holy Spirit." The doctrine of the
Trinity, therefore, expresses the mystery of the inner life
of the Godhead and at the same time retains, clarifies, and
purifies the profound truth contained in the Plotinian doctrine of emanation.

The living God, Who, in His tri-une reality, remains
shrouded in the darkness of unknowing, is nonetheless intimately present to the individual soul: by His grace He
dwells in the very substance of the soul and works toward
its sanctification and divinization. The soul is allowed to
seize His mysterious reality in pure and dark faith, and He
reveals Himself to the soul in a personal and existential relation and communication,

In this communication and communion the soul is
awakened, called to a new life, and endowed with new
capacities of both sense and spirit. The tri-une God, Who
enters into the soul in baptism, makes of it "a Temple of
the Holy Spirit" (John 14:23). These new capacities of the
soul are the three theological virtues, the gifts of the Holy
Spirit, which make the soul capable of understanding the
things of God, which, according to Scripture, God reveals
only to those who love Him.

In this mystical knowledge man realizes his true being,
by becoming what God wanted him to be when He created
him. And the same Word (*Logos*) by Whom everything
that is was created in the beginning, became incarnate in
the Son in order to atone for sin and redeem and renew
His creation. Owing to the mystery of Divine adoption, by
virtue of which man is called to become a friend of God
and a brother of Christ (cf. John 15:15), an intimacy between God and the individual soul has become possible
which could only be hopefully anticipated but not experienced or fully realized by the pre-Christian world.

The prime object in the life of a Christian is his growing assimilation to Christ, the model or archetype of the
human soul, which is to imitate this eternal pattern not only
externally, but internally by way of participation. And this

transformation of the soul in Christ is the work of the indwelling Holy Spirit (cf. John 14:23).

Natural mysticism, as has been pointed out, knows and speaks of the universal substantial presence of God in His creation, in every creature, and thus also in the human soul. This presence can be perceived by the natural light of reason. But the "experiential knowledge of God" of Christian mystics carries an entirely new and different meaning. Here God is present in the soul by virtue of the indwelling life of grace, and the mystical experience is the conscious awareness on the part of the soul of this presence. In the darkness of faith the hidden mystery of the Trinitarian life of God is revealed to the soul, which in a new and true sense has now become "an image and likeness of God." In its faith, in its hope, and in its love the soul here partakes of eternal life, in anticipation of the supreme bliss of the *beatific vision* in the life to come. In some measure the soul thus shares already in this life some of the treasures of the "Kingdom of Grace and Glory."

Grace and glory, however (according to traditional scholastic doctrine), do not destroy or efface nature but rather consecrate it and lead it to perfection. And the soul that has been raised to the state of perfection, enters, in the words of Ruysbroek, into "the kingdom of the beloved and of the loving. If anyone beholds this kingdom, God has placed him amidst the kingdom of the soul and into the pinnacle of the mind. This man has his place between a contemplative life resting in God and an emanating life spent in activity." This "pinnacle of the mind" is known by a variety of names in the history of Christian mysticism, such as *acumen* (*acies, intimum, summum sinus*) *mentis,* the *scintilla animae,* the little spark of the soul, the center of the soul, etc. All these expressions imply that here the spiritual soul is reunited with God its origin, and that this union is brought about by contemplating love. This contemplation is called *infused, extraordinary,* or *passive,* and it is essentially a *spiritual prayer* without apprehensions or images, that is, a purely spiritual prayer. It is this kind of contemplation of which St. John of the Cross treats in "The Dark (Passive) Night of the Spirit." To reach this state of perfection and mystical union, a special or extraordinary grace is required. Infused or passive contemplation, therefore, differs not only in degree but in essence from ordinary prayer and meditation or from what is termed *acquired, ordinary,* or *active contemplation.* This latter kind of prayer and meditation is discussed by St. John of the Cross in "The Ascent of Mount Carmel."

Infused contemplation differs from acquired contemplation as supernature differs from nature. It is called *passive* because the will and its affections have been completely silenced, so that the soul may become overt and wholly responsive to the promptings and gifts of God. According to Martin Grabmann, the ordinary Christian life consists in the active practice of the virtues, with the aid of sanctifying grace. It is carried on "in accordance with the rules of right reason." The life of mystical contemplation, on the other hand, depends on the initiative and action of the Holy Spirit and thus proceeds—in its highest stages —"in a supra-human or Divine manner" (*modo divino, ultra humanum modum* [Aquinas]).

The German mystics of the fourteenth century (notably Master Eckhardt, Suso, and Tauler) as well as the great Spanish mystics of the "Golden Age" (especially St. Theresa of Avila and St. John of the Cross) offer in their works a minute psychological description of these highest stages of the mystical life, although they point again and again to the difficulty of giving verbal expression to an experience that is ineffable. They emphasize in unison that in this sublime experience all the faculties are being spiritually transformed and actually divinized, so that man learns to live and walk in the presence of God. This life of perfect transformation and union in God, then, constitutes the third or "unitive way" of the mystical life.

In her book on the "mansions" of the "interior castle

of the soul" (*Las moradas*), St. Theresa enumerates three pre-mystical and four mystical "steps of prayer." The latter she calls the prayer of quiet, the prayer of union, the prayer of mystical betrothal, and the prayer of mystical marriage. At the height of mystical contemplation the human will is wholly conformed or "wedded" to the Divine will, so that the two wills or the two movements of love fuse and become one. Yet, according to the unanimous testimony of the great Christian mystics, even on this highest level of the mystical experience, in the "mystical union," the human soul retains its substantial independence: what takes place is not a union of human and Divine substances or natures, but a union of wills or a union of love. In this state the bodily senses re-enter into their rightful natural functions, and the union thus continues amidst the ordinary tasks and activities of daily life. In this highest mystical state there occurs finally also the fusion of understanding and love, of intellect and will, which are one in God. Visions, ecstasies, raptures, and all other preternatural phenomena are conspicuously absent on the highest levels of the mystical life.

It follows from what has been said that *infused contemplation* differs, on the one hand, from ordinary prayer and meditation and, on the other, from the "beatific vision." In his metaphor of the "secret ladder of love" St. John of the Cross distinguishes *ten steps* of mystical prayer, the last of which he describes as "the clear vision of God." To this vision, he says, "the soul which has ascended to the ninth step in this life, attains immediately after it has gone forth from the flesh" (cf. p. 216). Infused contemplation, therefore, may be designated as an *immediate* or direct knowledge when compared with discursive reasoning and meditation, but as *mediate* or *intermediate* when compared with the clarity of the "beatific vision."

Finally, it should be stressed that, on the basis of all the available evidence, genuine Christian mysticism is not hostile or foreign to the world and to nature. In Franciscan love it embraces the finite and temporal world of creatures, not, to be sure, as an end in itself, but as a means to the infinite and eternal. Inasmuch as the entire creation mirrors the Creator, all natural perfections point to the supernatural and supereminent perfection of God.

Elevated to the high state of mystical contemplation, the human soul is still (and more than ever) bound to perform humbly all the works of love; but it has become capable of performing them with a more collected intensity and with a higher degree of efficiency. In the words of Ruysbroek, "The works of love are commanded, whereas even supernatural contemplation would be defiled and destroyed without the works of love." For the Christian mystic, therefore, the active and the contemplative life are not contrasts but rather two intimately related and correlative forms of a fully integrated Christian life. And thus Christian mysticism is essentially nothing but the highest possible this-worldly development of the inherent spiritual capacity of the human soul.

Compared with the infinite plenitude of Divine Being, the creature is a mere nothing. Thus, when Ludwig Feuerbach, Friedrich Nietzsche, or Jean-Paul Sartre state in effect that, if God existed, He would of necessity "annihilate" man, they are not far from expressing a profound ontological and theological truth: inasmuch as God is Being in its fulness, all creaturely being derives from Him, and man can in truth claim nothing as his own. Since God alone is self-sufficient, it follows that before Him all creatures and the created world in its entirety are a mere nothing. And thus, the only thing which man can truly call his own is that nothingness from which God alone arouses him by His action at every instant of creaturely life. While the Being of God is absolute necessity, the being of all creatures is total contingency. In this sense it may well be said that "everything is grace." By recognizing his radical dependence on Divine grace, man simply acknowledges and accepts his condition as a creature of God. He exists as a creature to the extent that he is loved by his Creator. And he fulfills the meaning of his existence by accepting the Divine gifts of being, of goodness, and of love and by responding with the *élan* of his own love to the action and appeal of grace.

II. The Life and Work of St. John of the Cross

St. John of the Cross lived in an age of unrest and violent change, in the midst of those social and religious upheavals that marked the death-throes of the Middle Ages and the birth-throes of the modern world. The epoch was, on the one hand, rife with skeptical doubt, moral libertinism, and an iconoclastic frenzy and, on the other, filled with an as yet inarticulate longing for new spiritual guideposts that might aid in restoring order and balance to human existence.

Among the many reform movements of the sixteenth century the one initiated by the Spanish Cardinal Ximenes de Cisneros, the archbishop of Toledo, was undertaken along strictly orthodox lines. It preserved in the Iberian Peninsula the unity of the Catholic faith and thus spared the Spanish people the calamity of the religious schisms which were to disrupt other European nations for centuries to come. The *monastic reforms* of the sixteenth century, in Spain and elsewhere, were not merely symptoms of the rebirth of the spirit of Catholicism but the very source of its regained vitality and dynamic force.

In Spain the renascence of scholastic theology and philosophy and the new wave of mystical devotion coincided with the "Golden Age" of Spanish culture and literature. Thus the brilliance of style and artistic form that generally characterizes the great literary and artistic creations of the *siglo de oro* is reflected in the writings of the theologians, philosophers, and mystics.

The Spanish reform of ecclesiastic and monastic life achieved its most splendid successes through the heroic labors of St. Theresa of Avila and St. John of the Cross. Their writings are the immortal glory of Spanish literature and are surpassed in austere grandeur only by the timeless monuments of their lives. Both were members of the Order of Our Lady of Mount Carmel, which had been formally instituted about the middle of the twelfth century as an order of hermits on Mount Carmel in Palestine.

As their founder and "father" the Carmelites venerate the prophet Elias (9th cent., B.C.), who abolished in Israel the idolatrous cult of Baal, proclaimed Jahveh as the one living God, and re-established His worship among his people. In 1206 A.D., St. Albert, Patriarch of Jerusalem, gave the Carmelites their first monastic rule. When, in the course of the thirteenth century, the order made its first appearance in Europe, its members tried to combine the austere life of the early hermits of the eastern deserts with the missionary zeal of the newly founded Mendicant Orders. They vied with Franciscans and Dominicans in their efforts to enkindle in the hearts of the people a special devotion to the Virgin Mary and were therefore commonly known as the "Brethren of Our Lady."

In 1432, the original Carmelite rule of St. Albert was mitigated by Pope Eugenius IV, and the Reform of the sixteenth century was in the main a protest against this relaxation of Carmelite discipline and an attempt to restore the full rigor of a cloistered contemplative life.

In closest collaboration St. Theresa and St. John of the Cross carried the Reform to a successful conclusion. They did so in the face of the most violent opposition on the part of the advocates of the Mitigated Observance. Undergoing incredible hardships and overcoming almost insuperable obstacles, they introduced the original rule of St. Albert into many of the established communities and founded numerous new ones. Their extraordinary understanding of human souls was the fruit of a rare combination of spiritual inwardness, sober practical sense, and a sustained force of will.

As to St. John of the Cross, in his significance as a profound Christian thinker and a great poet he far transcends the boundaries of his country and his age. As a theologian and mystical writer he succeeded in impressing the severe beat of his life upon the lapidary style of his works. He was a contemplative with a sensitive artistic mind, and his strangely "surrealistic" drawing of the crucified Christ shows an immediacy and spontaneity of expression that have evoked the admiration of contemporary artists (such as Salvador Dali) and art critics.

Juan de Yepes (who later on adopted the name Juan de la Cruz) was born at Fontiveros near Avila, in the southern part of old Castile. He was the youngest of three sons. His brother Francisco lived to testify during the initial stages of his brother's process of beatification. His father was a member of the lower nobility, but he had been cast off by his family when he had married Catalina Alvarez, who was poor and of humble parentage. When John's father died, Catalina found herself and her small children without even the bare necessities of life.

Looking for more favorable conditions of work, the widow moved to the village of Arévalo and shortly afterwards to the town of Medina del Campo. There John was apprenticed in the workshops of some of the local artisans and craftsmen. Although he could thus make his modest contribution to the support of his family, his successive attempts at carpentering, tailoring, carving, and painting left him discontented. He served as an acolyte at a local convent of Augustinian nuns and received his first formal religious and secular education at the College of the Children of Doctrine, a convent school for the children of the poor.

The deep piety and humility of the young altar boy attracted the attention of Don Alonso Alvarez of Toledo, a devout nobleman and a friend and protector of the poor. He had recently founded a smallpox hospital at Medina del Campo. Don Alonso believed he recognized in John a religious vocation, and he therefore persuaded the boy's mother to permit her son to become an attendant at the hospital. On the side, in the spare moments which his care of the sick left him, John began his studies for the priest-hood. According to Don Alonso's plan, his protégé was to become the chaplain of the hospital after his ordination.

In 1553, the Fathers of the recently founded Jesuit Order had established one of their colleges at Medina del Campo, and in 1555 John was sent to that already re-nowned institution of higher learning to continue his studies, while at the same time he continued to attend to the sick at the hospital. At the Jesuit college he completed his educa-tion in Latin and in the liberal arts.

John was twenty-one years of age when, in 1563, he entered the novitiate of the Carmelite Order in the local college of St. Anne, one of the numerous Carmelite houses of study. The prospect of becoming the hospital's chaplain held no longer any attraction for him. He was determined never to accept any office or dignity that might detract him from total dedication to God.

When the novice received the habit of the Carmelite Order he was given the name of John of Saint Mathias. In 1564, the young scholastic was sent to the Carmelite college of St. Andrew at Salamanca to finish his studies in theology and philosophy. Salamanca was at that time the center of Thomistic thought and was widely renowned as "the Athens of Christendom." It was at Salamanca that John acquired the thorough knowledge of the principles of scholastic the-ology and philosophy of which there is such ample evidence in his writings.

In 1576, John was appointed "master of students" and commissioned to lecture to the scholastics of the Carmelite college. Ordained a priest in the same year, he returned to Medina del Campo and there celebrated his first mass. Shortly afterwards he met Mother Theresa who had come to Medina del Campo to found one of the convents of the Carmelite Reform. For both saints and for the future course of the Reform this meeting had far-reaching consequences.

Despite the fact that after his profession in the Carmelite Order John had been given special permission to live according to the primitive rule of the Carmel, it now appeared that the cloistered monastic life did not fully satisfy his longing for solitude, austerity, and heroic discipline. At any rate, he intimated to his superiors that it was his intention to become a Carthusian monk and that he hoped to be received into the Carthusian settlement of Paular in Segovia. Mother Theresa, however, succeeded in persuading him to defer a final decision in this matter. So John returned to Salamanca for another year.

Mother Theresa had been offered a small farmhouse in the hamlet of Duruelo, in the vicinity of Medina del Campo. It was little more than a shack, but for John it had all the attractions he could have wished for: the place was lonely and desolate, the climate severe, and he could live there in absolute poverty and practise total detachment. This ramshackle farmhouse thus became the first monastery of the Theresian Reform. Seven friars in all, the vanguard of the Reform, were joined together in the little Carmelite community at Duruelo.

John and his companions, at Duruelo as at all times, joined action to contemplation, preaching and teaching in the neighboring villages. And since the demands were heavy and the laborers in the apostolic work so few, John asked his mother and his brother Francisco with his wife to move into the hermitage of Duruelo to lend a helping hand. When, after a year and a half, the place proved definitely too small to house the growing community, the friars gratefully accepted the more spacious quarters which had been offered to them in the neighboring town of Mancera. John had been appointed master of novices at Duruelo and he continued in the same office at Mancera and, two years later, in the newly founded monastery at Pastrana. In 1571, he founded a Carmelite college at Alcalà de Henares and became its first Rector.

In 1572, Theresa was made Prioress of the Convent of the Incarnation at Avila, one of the largest communities of Carmelite nuns of the Mitigated Observance and one in which laxity and worldliness were quite conspicuous. Almost immediately Theresa called on John of the Cross to aid her in the difficult task of leading the nuns back to the strict Carmelite way of life. Though twenty-seven years younger than Mother Theresa, John became her spiritual director and one of the two confessors of the one hundred and thirty nuns of the convent.

Meanwhile, storm clouds had been gathering, threatening with destruction the still fragile tree of the Reform. During the night of the third of December, 1577, Carmelites of the Mitigated Observance seized John of the Cross and took him to Toledo as their prisoner. A General Chapter of the Order, convoked at Piacenza in 1575, had virtually outlawed the advocates of the Reform as dangerous innovators and rebels who must be subdued by force, if necessary. They were to be compelled to rejoin the communities of the Mitigated Observance.

In the Carmelite monastery at Toledo, John found himself face to face with Father Tostado, a learned and energetic Carmelite of the Mitigated Observance, who tried every means of persuasion to make the saint renounce the Reform. John's refusal to do so was taken as a sign of malicious obstinacy and disobedience, and he was thereupon imprisoned in the monastery. His cell was about ten feet long and six feet wide and so low "that he could hardly stand erect, even though he was very short in stature," as Mother Theresa wrote later on. In this airless and windowless dungeon the prisoner was to spend almost nine months. But after John had finally regained his freedom, he called his jailers "his great benefactors," adding that never before had he received "such a plenitude of supernatural light and consolation." But whenever he was asked to recant and to renounce the Reform, he showed himself "immovable as a rock."

John's abduction and incarceration had taken place in deepest secrecy. Mother Theresa was entirely in the dark as to the saint's whereabouts. Her urgent letters to King

Philip II produced no results. Meanwhile, John was leading a "hidden life" in more than one sense. He was hidden from his friends and hidden in the love of God, which now bore down on him heavily, demanding that total surrender of self which marks "the narrow road" that leads to Life. He was finally given what he had so ardently desired, "sufferings to be borne for Thy sake, and that I may be despised and counted for nothing." The "Doctor of Nothingness" (*El doctor de la nada*) had come into his own.

Cut off from all human consolation and—to increase his suffering—also from the sacramental life of the Church, John's body was slowly wasting away, but his spirit was drawn to the eternal source of light and love. In the darkness and abandonment of his prison, his soul began to chant the songs of the *Spiritual Canticle*. In the dark nights of Toledo the ancient theme of the bridal song of the human soul—the Song of Songs—was born anew in his heart. The Spouse of Christ experiences her betrothal to the Divine Bridegroom as the eternal paradigm of all human and finite bridal relationship. It was in his prison cell at Toledo that John composed the first thirty stanzas of the *Spiritual Canticle*. They tell of the way to the heavenly light that leads through the fearful "passive nights of the spirit." And this way of the Cross is the true way of Life, because for those whose love follows their Master into the darkest night of total abandonment, suffering turns into bliss, death into life, night into light.

The story of John's almost miraculous escape is well authenticated and makes exciting reading. The flight was carefully planned and executed without any human help and in the face of overwhelming odds. Out of strips torn from two old blankets and a tunic, he fashioned a sort of rope and, after having managed to unscrew the heavy locks of his cell and of the adjoining hall, he let himself down through a window high up in the gallery overlooking the river Tagus. From the heights of the ramparts of Toledo he leaped into the darkness and found himself unhurt in the patio outside the enclosure of the Franciscan Convent of the Conception.

The following day John arrived completely exhausted at the convent of the Carmelite nuns of the Reform, where he was given temporary shelter. Again a few days later he found refuge at Holy Cross Hospital, the administrator of which was Don Pedro Gonzales de Mendoza, the influential canon and treasurer of the Church of Toledo.

With the death of Father Rubeo, the Superior General of the Carmelites of the Mitigated Observance (in May, 1578), the storms of persecution subsided. The next immediate goal of Mother Theresa and John of the Cross was to bring about the complete administrative separation of the two branches of the Order, but, for the time being, all these efforts remained unsuccessful. The Papal Nuncio issued a decree which placed the houses of the Reform under the jurisdiction of the Mitigated Observance.

At the General Chapter meeting of the reformed members of the Order (October, 1578), John of the Cross was appointed Prior of the *Calvario,* a monastery located in the vicinity of Beas de Segura. It was here that the saint wrote the commentaries on his *Spiritual Canticle* and in all probability also his treatises on *The Ascent to Mount Carmel* and *The Dark Night of the Soul.*

John was now in his thirty-seventh year. In 1579, he assumed the rectorship of the Carmelite college at Baeza. This cultural center of Andalusia was a city with a university renowned for its contributions to scriptural studies. In the two years he spent there, the saint worked out in great detail the rules and principles which were to guide the future establishments of the Reform.

A Brief issued by Pope Gregory XIII in June, 1580, made it possible for the communities of the Reform to elect their own Provincial and thereby to establish their independence. In the following year John was appointed Prior of the monastery of *Los Mártires* at Granada. This house had been founded as early as 1573 and derived its name from the fact that it was located at the site where formerly the Moorish Kings of Granada had held their Christian captives. It was in the picturesque setting of this Andalusian city with its impressive monuments of Christian and Moslem culture that John of the Cross completed most of his works, and it was here that his spiritual direction of souls bore its richest fruits.

At the Provincial Chapter of the year 1585 John was named Provincial Vicar of Andalusia, and during the following years he founded new houses of the Reform at Córdoba, Sevilla, Madrid, Manchuela, and Caravaca. With the election of Father Nicolás Doria as Vicar General of the reformed branch of the Order, in June, 1588, new difficulties, arising from conflicting views among the leaders of the Reform, began to threaten further consolidation. For John of the Cross this meant a recurrence of persecution and suffering. Thus the favors he had asked for the declining years of his life, he now received: "Not to die as a prelate; to die at a place where he was not even known; and to die after having suffered much."

In 1588, John was named Prior of the Carmelite monastery in Segovia. Here his contemplative life reached its greatest heights, although already at Granada, according to his own testimony, he had experienced the grace of "mystical union." The Chapter of 1591 stripped John of all his offices and forbade him any kind of activity in the Order. There was even talk of expelling him from the Carmelite community. But it was finally decided to send him into the solitude of Peñuela in the Sierra Morena. There he became seriously ill. When his condition made it necessary to move him to another place, he was given the choice between Baeza and Ubeda. At Baeza was the college which he had founded and whose first Rector he had been. There he had friends who would understand him and care for him. Ubeda was a new foundation, headed by Father Francis

Chrysostome, one of his fiercest opponents. By choosing Ubeda, the saint gave living testimony to what he had taught in the *Ascent to Mount Carmel:*

> Take care that you always choose not the easiest, but the hardest. . . . Desire nothing but to enter for Christ's sake into total nakedness, emptiness and poverty with respect to all the things of this world.

In this spirit of total detachment, John, seated on the little mule which a friend had put at his disposal, began his last earthly journey. For days he had been unable to take any food or drink. His swollen leg was covered with festering sores and open wounds. In silence the little friar and his patient beast of burden travelled over the seven miles of mountainous road to his new destination.

At Ubeda the dying man was given the poorest and smallest cell. The attending physician resorted to surgery, but the infection spread rapidly. In the night from Friday, December 13th to Saturday, 1591, on hearing the familiar sound of the bell that called the community to arise for the prayer of matins, John pronounced his last words: "Into Thy hands, oh Lord, I commend my spirit."

John of the Cross was beatified on January 25th, 1675, and canonized on December 26, 1726.

III. The Texts

As Father Silverio de Santa Teresa of the Carmelite Order states in the introduction to our texts in his critical edition of the works of St. John of the Cross, the "Ascent to Mount Carmel" and "The Dark Night" form in reality *one* coherent mystical treatise, and the traditional separation is more or less accidental and artificial. The *Dark Night* is a continuation and complement of the *Ascent,* as the author himself explains when he writes: "The *first night* or purgation is the night of the sensual part of the soul, which . . .

will be considered in the *first part* of this book. The *second night* is the night of the spiritual part of the soul, and of this we treat . . . throughout the *second and third* parts— as far as the *active role* of the soul is concerned. *Passive or infused contemplation* will be considered in the *fourth part"* (Ascent, Book I, chap. 1).

The first draft of the *Ascent* was begun at *El Calvario* and probably rewritten and completed in its present fragmentary form at Granada. Unfortunately, the original manuscripts are lost; but some of the existing early copies have been made with great care and are therefore regarded as completely reliable. The text of the *Dark Night* is likewise fragmentary, but the gap is to some extent filled by some of the other mystical writings of the saint, especially the *Spiritual Canticle* and *The Living Flame of Love*. Here, too, the original manuscripts are lost, but all of the extant twelve early copies are accurate and reliable.

K.F.R.

SELECTED BIBLIOGRAPHY

Obras de San Juan de la Cruz. Editadas y anotadas por el
P. Silverio de Santa Teresa, O.C.D. (Burgos, 1929-
1931), 5 vols.

Complete Works. Translated and edited by E. Allison Peers
(Westminster: Newman, 1953), 3 vols.

P. Bruno de Jésus-Marie, O.C.D. *St. John of the Cross*.
Edited by Fr. Benedict Zimmerman, O.C.D. With an
Introduction by Jacques Maritain (New York: Ben-
ziger, 1932).

P. Gabriel of St. Mary Magdalen, O.C.D. *St. John of the
Cross* (Westminster: Newman, 1946).

Frost, Bede. *St. John of the Cross* (London: Hodder and
Stoughton, 1937).

Merton, Thomas. *The Ascent to Truth* (New York: Har-
court, Brace and Company, 1951).

CONTENTS

PART I
The Ascent to Mount Carmel

BOOK ONE
The First Dark Night of Sense and Desire

BOOK TWO
The First Dark Night of the Spirit: Faith

BOOK THREE
The First Dark Night of the Spirit: Hope and Love

PART II
The Passive Night of the Soul

BOOK ONE
The Night of Sense

BOOK TWO
The Night of the Spirit

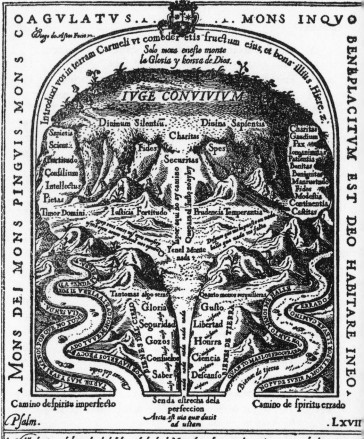

The Ascent to Mount Carmel ("The Mount of Perfection") reproduced from the main Spanish edition, slightly reduced

PART I*

THE ASCENT TO MOUNT CARMEL

*The main theme and final goal: the soul's union
with God.*

This treatise deals with the manner in which a soul may
prepare itself to attain to union with God. It gives useful
advice and instruction, both to beginners and to those more
advanced in the spiritual life, so that they may learn how to
free themselves from all that is temporal and not weigh
themselves down with the spiritual, and remain in that complete nakedness and freedom of the spirit which are necessary for union with God.

The entire doctrine which I intend to discuss in the
Ascent to Mount Carmel is contained in the following
stanzas, and they describe also the manner of ascending to
the peak of the mountain, that is, that high state of perfection which we here designate as the union of the soul
with God. The poem reads as follows:

1

In a dark night,
My longing heart aglow with love,
—Oh, blessed lot!—
I went forth unseen
From my house that was at last in deepest rest.

2

Secure and protected by darkness,

* The text of "The Ascent to Mount Carmel" and "The Dark
Night of the Soul" has been reduced to approximately one third the
length of the originals, without sacrificing continuity of thought. The
chapter headings and sectional subheadings have in many instances
been lengthened and made more descriptive for the benefit of the
reader.—*The Editor and Translator.*

I climbed the secret ladder, in disguise,
—Oh, blessed lot!—
In darkness, veiled and concealed I went
Leaving behind my house in deepest rest.

3

Oh, blissful night!
Oh, secret night, when I remained unseeing and unseen,
When the flame burning in my heart
Was my only light and guide.

4

This inward light,
A safer guide than noonday's brightness,
Showed me the place where He awaited me
—My soul's Beloved—
A place of solitude.

5

Oh, night that guided me!
Oh, night more lovely than the rosy dawn!
Oh, night whose darkness guided me
To that sweet union,
In which the lover and Beloved are made one.

6

Upon the flower of my breast,
Kept undefiled for Him alone,
He fell asleep,
While I was waking,
Caressing Him with gentle cedars' breeze.

7

And when Aurora's breath
Began to spread His curled hair,
His gentle hand

He placed upon my neck,
And all my senses were in bliss suspended.

8

Forgetful of myself,
My head reclined on my Beloved,
The world was gone
And all my cares at rest,
Forgotten all my grief among the lilies.

Prologue

The ascent through the dark night is an extraordinary way and requires extraordinary understanding on the part of the soul's directors.

To explain and make intelligible the nature of this dark night, through which the soul passes on its way to the Divine light of that perfect union—the most perfect possible in this life—which may reward the love of God, it would be necessary to have another and greater light of knowledge and experience than my own; for so manifold and so profound are the darknesses and trials—both spiritual and temporal—through which those blessed souls must pass in order to attain to this high state of perfection that no mere human knowledge suffices to understand them; nor does any ordinary experience suffice to describe them. Only he who himself travels this way can have an inner awareness of it, but even he cannot express it adequately in words.

In my attempt, therefore, to tell something about this dark night, I shall put my trust neither in experience nor in knowledge, since both may fail and deceive; rather, while availing myself as much as possible of the aid of personal experience and knowledge, I shall make use of Holy Scripture in everything that, with Divine help, I may be able to say; for, since He Who speaks therein is the Holy Ghost, we cannot possibly go astray. And if nonetheless I should be in error, it was certainly not my intention to deviate in any point from the sound sense and doctrine of our Holy Mother, the Catholic Church. I submit and resign myself not only to her command, but to her better reason and judgment.

It is sad to see many souls, whom God favors with sufficient gifts of mind for making progress, remaining in a rudimentary stage of communion with God, either because of weakness of will or lack of knowledge, or because there is no one to lead them on the right path and to teach them how to move on from these beginnings. For though it is true that God is leading them and that He can lead them even without their own endeavor, they often will not allow themselves to be thus led. There are souls who, instead of surrendering their own selves to God, rather impede God's activity by their imprudent behavior and their resistance.

And thus, in order that all—whether they are beginners or already advanced in their spiritual life—may learn, when His Majesty wants to lead them onward, how to entrust themselves to His guidance, we shall, with His help, offer instruction and counsel, so that these souls may be able to discern God's intention, or, at least, allow Him to lead them. For some confessors and spiritual directors, owing to the fact that they have no light and experience in these ways of the spiritual life, are prone to hinder and harm such souls rather than help them on this road. It is likely to happen that God may lead the soul by a most lofty path of dark contemplation and spiritual aridity, wherein the soul believes itself to be completely lost. Such a soul, being filled with darkness, misery, afflictions, and temptations, will perhaps then meet someone who speaks to it like Job's comforters, telling it that it is suffering from melancholy or despair, or from a morbid condition of mind, or that the cause of its affliction must be some hidden guilt, and that for this reason God has abandoned it. And such inexperienced counsellors will then immediately jump to the conclusion that this soul must harbor great evil, since it is afflicted by such things.

And there will be those also who will tell this soul to turn back, since it is finding neither joy nor consolation in the things of God as it did prior to this present state. But by giving such advice they merely double the trials of this poor soul; for it may well be that the greatest affliction which it feels is the knowledge of its own misery. It seems to such a soul that its view of its own self reveals clearer than daylight that it is filled with evils and sins, for, as we shall soon have occasion to show, God gives the soul this light of self-knowledge in that night of contemplation. And the type of confessors we have in mind, suspecting that such afflictions of the soul are caused by sin, make these souls examine and re-examine their past lives, demanding that they make many general confessions, and in this manner they cause them ever renewed torment. They do not understand that this is perhaps not the proper time to use any such methods, but that these souls should rather be left in the state of purgation in which God has placed them.

In subsequent chapters of this treatise we shall, with Divine aid, consider these matters; and we shall discuss also in what manner the soul should behave in such a situation, and how the confessor should deal with it, and what signs there are whereby it may be known if this state of purgation is genuine. If such is the case, it will then be necessary to determine whether it is a purgation of sense or of spirit and how it may be known that we are not dealing with a state of melancholy or some other imperfection of either sense or spirit. Again, there are many souls who think they have lost the spirit of prayer, when in reality their prayer has gained in depth; and there are others who think themselves far advanced in the spirit of prayer, when in reality their prayer amounts to little more than nothing.

Inasmuch as this instruction deals with the dark night through which the soul must pass on its way to God, the reader should not be too much surprised if the teaching appears somewhat dark to him also. And if some persons find themselves in disagreement with this teaching, they should blame my imperfect knowledge and poor style; for the doctrine as such is sound and of the greatest importance.

It is not my main intention to address all and sundry, but rather to speak in a very special manner to certain members of our sacred Order of Mount Carmel of the primitive observance—both friars and nuns—since they have asked me to do so. I have in mind those in particular to whom

God is granting the favor of setting them on the path to this Mountain. Since they are already detached from the temporal things of this world, they will have a better understanding of the doctrine of the emptiness and detachment of the spirit.

BOOK ONE

The First Dark Night of Sense and Desire

CHAPTER ONE

The two nights through which spiritual persons pass.

THE FIRST STANZA

In a dark night,
My heart aglow with love,
—Oh, blessed lot!—
I went forth unseen
From my house that was at last in deepest rest.

If a soul aspires to the state of perfection, it must ordinarily first pass through two principal kinds of night, which spiritual writers call purgations or purifications of the soul; here we call them nights, because in both of them the soul walks, as it were, in night or in darkness.

The *first night* or purgation is the night of the *sensual* part of the soul, which is referred to in the present stanza and which will be further considered throughout the first part of this book. The *second night* is the night of the *spiritual* part of the soul, and of this we treat in the second stanza and throughout the second and third parts—as far as the *active* role of the soul is concerned; *passive* or *infused contemplation* will be considered in the fourth part.

The first night is experienced by beginners in the spiritual life; it occurs at the time when God first places them in the state of contemplation. The second night or purification is experienced by persons more advanced in the spiritual life, at the time when it pleases God to raise them to the

9

state of union with Him. And this latter night is a darker and more terrible purgation.

Preliminary explanation of the stanza.

In this first stanza, then, the soul means, in short, to say that (led by God) it went forth, solely motivated by its love for Him; that, aglow with love for Him, it went forth in a dark night. And this dark night signifies that the soul has emptied and purged itself of all its sense appetites regarding the external things of the world, of all desire for carnal pleasure, and also of all the gratifications of its will. This is why the soul says that it went forth while its house lay in stillness or was at rest. The house signifies the sensual part of the soul: the desires are stilled and asleep in the soul, and the soul in them. For the soul is unable to go forth from the pains and anxieties of the secret hiding places of the sense appetites unless these latter are first subdued and put to sleep. And, the soul says, it was a blessed lot to go thus forth in silence and secrecy, without being seen, that is, without being hindered and disturbed by any carnal desire or anything else. And the soul went forth by night, which means that God had deprived it of all these things, and this privation was night for it.

CHAPTER II

"In a dark night."
Night of sense and night of faith.

There are three reasons which justify us to speak of this journey of the soul to ultimate union with God as of a passage through the night. The first relates to the soul's point of departure; for, by denying to itself all those things of the world which it possessed, it must step by step free itself from all desire for them; and this denial and loss are as night to all the senses of man. The second reason refers to the manner or mode of the soul's journey toward this union; for it travels along the road of faith, which is likewise as dark as night to the understanding. The third reason, finally, has to do with the goal or end toward which the soul travels; and this end is God, Who also is like a dark night to the soul in this life.

These three kinds of night are, however, all one night. Yet, like night itself, this night has three parts. The first part—the night of sense—is comparable to the beginning of night. The second part—the night of faith—may be compared to midnight, which is total darkness. And the third part is like the end of night or the early dawn, that is, close to the light of day or close to the Divine light.

CHAPTER III

The primary causes of this night are desire and attachment.

We here call night the deprivation of all delight that derives from the desire of things; for as night is but the absence of light, and, consequently, a disappearance of all objects that can be seen by means of light, whereby the faculty of sight remains in darkness and without any object, so also the quelling of desire may be called a night of the soul, since the soul remains in darkness and without any object when it is deprived of the pleasure derived from its desire of things. Just as the visual power is nourished and fed by objects which can be seen, and which are not seen when the light is extinguished, so the soul, by its desire, is nourished and fed by all things in which it can take pleasure according to its powers or faculties. And when this desire is quenched, or rather, silenced, then the soul ceases to feed upon its pleasure in all things and thus remains in darkness and without any object. We may therefore say that the soul that has denied and cast away the pleasure in all things, and has silenced its desire for them, remains as in the darkness of night: it has emptied itself of all things.

The reason for this is, that, as the philosophers tell us, the soul, when God infuses it into the body, is like a plain and empty slate (*tabula rasa*), on which nothing is depicted or inscribed; and, aside from that which it learns to know by means of the senses, nothing is communicated to it, in the course of nature, from any other source. Nor could the soul, in the course of nature, acquire any knowledge in any way except by means of the senses, which are the windows of its prison.

If then the soul rejects and denies admission to that which it is able to receive through the senses, we may well say that it remains, as it were, in darkness and emptiness. Although it is true that the soul cannot really cease to hear, to see, to smell, to taste, and to touch, this is no longer of great importance; nor is the soul which rejects and denies admission to the objects of sense any more encumbered by these objects than if it saw them not, heard them not, and so on. Just as he who shuts his eyes is as much in darkness as the blind man who lacks the faculty of sight. The saying of David, "I am poor and in labors from the time of my youth," seems quite appropriate in this regard. David calls himself poor, although it is clear that he was rich; but his will was not attached to his riches, and so it was as though he was really poor. If, on the other hand, he had been really poor and had not been poor or detached in his will, he would not have been truly poor; for then his soul would have been filled to overflowing with desire. We are, then, not speaking here of the lack of things, for such an external deprivation is not the true nakedness of detachment as long as the soul retains its desire for things; we rather do mean that nakedness which liberates the soul from its pleasure in things and from its desire for them—a nakedness which leaves the soul free and void of things, although it may have them. What possesses and harms the soul is not the things of this world but rather the will and desire for them;

for what enters into the soul and dwells in it is not things but the desire for things.

CHAPTER IV

The dark night is the silencing of desire and spiritual poverty.

The reason why it is necessary for the soul, in order to attain to union with God, to pass through this dark night is that all the affections which the soul has for creatures are pure darkness in the eyes of God. As long as the soul is clothed in these affections it lacks the capacity for being enlightened and permeated by the pure and simple light of God; for light cannot coexist with darkness. As St. John (1:5) says: *"Tenebrae eam non comprehenderunt."* That is: The darkness could not receive the light.

Philosophy teaches us that two contraries cannot coexist in one and the same subject. Thus, darkness, which is affection for creatures, and light, which is God, are opposites, and there is no likeness or conformity between them; as St. Paul told the Corinthians when he said: "What is there in common between light and darkness?" (2 Cor. 6:14)

The affection and attachment which the soul has for creatures makes it like unto these creatures, and the greater the affection, the closer will be the equality and resemblance between them. For love creates a likeness between that which loves and that which is loved. And thus, he who loves a creature becomes as low as that creature, and, in a way, even lower; for love makes the lover not only equal to that which he loves but even subjects him to it. And this is why the soul which loves anything (aside from God) renders itself incapable of pure Divine union and of transformation in God. For the lowliness of the creature is much less capable of attaining to the exalted height of the Creator than darkness is capable of attaining to light. Compared with

God, all the things of earth and heaven are nothing. In this sense, then, all creatures are nothing; and we may add that their affections are less than nothing, since they are an impediment to the creature's transformation in God.

All the being of creatures, compared with the infinite Being of God, is nothing. And therefore the soul whose affections cling to creatures is likewise nothing and less than nothing before God. This is why such a soul will in no wise be able to be united with the infinite Being of God; for that which is not can have no share in that which is. And all the beauty of creatures, compared with the infinite Beauty of God, is nothing but ugliness. The soul, therefore, whose affections are attached to the beauty of any creature is greatly deformed in the eyes of God. And such a deformed soul is incapable of being transformed into the Beauty of God; for ugliness can have no share in beauty. And all the goodness of the creatures of the world, compared with the infinite Goodness of God, can be called iniquity; for nothing is good, except God alone (Luke 18:19). The soul, therefore, which sets its heart upon worldly goods is supremely evil in the eyes of God. And as iniquity has no comprehension of goodness, so such a soul cannot be united with God, Who is supreme goodness. Again, all the wisdom of the world and all human accomplishments, compared with the infinite Wisdom of God, are total and supreme ignorance; as St. Paul writes in the Epistle to the Corinthians: "The wisdom of this world is foolishness in the eyes of God" (1 Cor. 3:19).

Those alone can attain to the Wisdom of God who, like ignorant children, lay aside their knowledge and walk in His service with love. And all worldly dominion and worldly freedom, compared with the dominion and freedom of the spirit of God, are nothing but serfdom, anguish, and captivity. And a soul [in such captivity] will be unable to attain to that true freedom of spirit which is granted in this Divine union. For slavery can have no part in freedom; and freedom cannot dwell in a heart that is subject to desires, since such a heart is that of a slave. Freedom dwells in the heart of the free man, for his heart is that of a son.

And all the delights and gratifications which the will finds in the things of this world, in comparison with the delights found in God, are great affliction, torment, and bitterness. He who sets his heart upon these is therefore, in the sight of God, judged deserving of great affliction, torment, and bitterness and will thus be unable to attain to the delights of the embrace of union with God. And again, all the riches and glory of created things and beings, compared with the wealth that is God, are utter poverty and misery. The soul, then, which loves and possesses such creaturely riches is exceedingly poor and wretched in the eyes of God and for this reason will be unable to attain to that richness and glory which are found in the state of transformation in God.

CHAPTER V

The distance between creatures in themselves and God in Himself.

From what has been said it may be seen in some measure how great is the distance between what creatures are in themselves and what God is in Himself, and why souls which are attached in their affections to any of these creatures are equally far removed from God. And thus he who desires to love anything together with God certainly esteems God very little, since he attaches equal weight to that which, as we have said, is so far removed from God. Inasmuch, then, as there is nothing that is equal with God, the soul which loves or clings to some other thing together with Him, offends Him greatly. And if this is the case, what shall we say of a soul that loves anything more than God?

CHAPTER VI

*Desire darkens and weakens the soul and deprives it
of the spirit of God.*

In order that what we have said may be more clearly and
fully understood, it will be well here to explain in what way
the desires [for the goods of this world] cause two main
evils in the soul. The one is that they deprive the soul of
the spirit of God, and the other is that they weary, torment,
darken, defile, and weaken the soul in which they dwell.
These two evils—the one privative or negative, the other
positive—have as their cause any disordered act of desire.

First, speaking of the privative, it is clear that, owing
to the fact that the soul attaches its affections to a thing
pertaining to the category of creature, the more this desire
fills the soul, the less capacity it will have for the Creator.
For, as the philosophers tell us, two contraries cannot exist
in one and the same subject, and love of God and affection
for creatures are contraries, so that there cannot be room in
one will for a love of creatures and the love of God. In
the measure, therefore, in which the soul is subjected to the
spirit of sense, the purely spiritual cannot enter into it.

Secondly, these desires weary, torment, darken, defile,
and weaken the soul; and we shall in the following discuss
these five things, one by one.

Regarding the first, it is clear that the desires weary
and exasperate the soul, for they are like restless and discontented children, who are ever demanding one thing or
another from their mother, and are never satisfied. And as
one who greedily digs for a treasure is wearied and exhausted, so is the soul wearied and exhausted if it chases
after those things which its desires demand of it. And it is
never satisfied. It is wounded, stirred up and driven hither
and thither by its desires as is water by gusts of wind. Speak-

ing of such a soul, Isaiah says: "The heart of the wicked man is like a raging sea" (Is. 29:8). And a wicked man indeed is he who subdues not his desires.

CHAPTER VII

The desires torment the soul.

The second kind of positive evil which the desires cause in the soul is that they torment and hurt it after the manner of one who is tormented by being bound with ropes. And of this David says: "The cords of my sins (which are my desires) have constrained me round about" (Ps. 118:61). For the desires take hold of the soul, wounding it and causing it pain and distress like so many thorns. And the more intense the desire, the greater the torment which it causes in the soul.

But while creatures cause torment, the spirit of God makes the soul rejoice. And thus God calls to us through the mouth of St. Matthew: "Come to Me, all you who labor and are burdened, and I will refresh you; and you shall find rest for your souls" (Matt. 11:28-29). As though he were to say: All you who go about tormented, afflicted and weighed down by your cares and desires, leave all these behind, come to Me that I may refresh you and you may find for your souls the rest which your desires take from you.

CHAPTER VIII

The desires make the soul blind.

The third evil which the desires cause in the soul is that they darken it and make it blind. David, speaking of this matter, says: "My iniquities have taken hold of me, and I have lost my power of sight" (Ps. 6:4). And when the soul is thus darkened in its understanding, it is also blunted in its will, and the faculty of memory becomes dull and disordered in its proper functions. For, as these latter faculties in their operations depend on the understanding, it is clear that, when the understanding is blurred, they too will become disordered and disturbed. The understanding, after all, has no more capacity for being illumined by the Wisdom of God than has the air in the darkness of night for receiving light from the sun; nor has the will any power to embrace God in pure love, even as a mirror that is clouded with vapor has no power to reflect clearly an object; and even less power has the memory that is dimmed by the darkness of desire for receiving a clear impression of the image of God, even as muddy water cannot show forth clearly the face of a person who looks at his own reflection therein.

Desire thus makes the soul dark and blind; for desire, as such, is blind. And this is the reason why, whenever the soul allows itself to be guided by its desires, it becomes blind also. It may then be compared to a person who can see but allows himself to be guided by one who is unable to see, which is as bad as if both were blind. And what follows from this is precisely what Our Lord tells us through the mouth of St. Matthew: "When one blind man leads another, both will fall into the ditch" (Matt. 15:14).

This, then, is what desire does to the soul: it kindles its concupiscence and blurs its understanding, so that it can no longer see its own light. One must therefore greatly deplore the ignorance of some persons, who burden themselves with excessive penances and many other voluntary exercises, thinking this or that particular practice will suffice to procure for them the union with Divine Wisdom. This is by no means the case unless they first diligently endeavor to silence their desires. If they would take care to spend half the amount of their labor on this endeavor, they would derive more benefit therefrom in a month than they do from all those other exertions in many years. The soul will surely not rid itself of its darkness and coarseness until its desires are silenced; for they are like cataracts, or like motes in the eye, which obstruct the vision until they are removed.

CHAPTER IX

The desires defile the soul.

The fourth harm which is done to the soul by the desires is that they tarnish and defile it. As traces of soot will tarnish a beautiful and perfectly formed face, so inordinate desires cause a soul in which they live to become ugly and un-clean—a soul which in itself is a most beautiful and per-fectly formed image of God.

All this evil, and even more, is caused in the soul by its inordinate desires for the things of this world; so much so that, if we were trying to describe the ugly and unclean appearance which the desires can give the soul, we should find nothing, not even the decomposition of a corpse, nor anything else that is impure and defiled, with which we could compare it. For, though it is true that the disordered soul, in its natural [metaphysical] substance, is as perfect as when God created it, in its rational [moral] mode of being it has become ugly, impure, black, and saturated with all the evils which are here described, and many more. What I am saying and what I cannot emphasize enough in connection with my purpose, is that any desire, even though it were only a matter of the least imperfection, tarnishes the soul and makes it impure.

CHAPTER X

The desires make the soul tepid.

The fifth way in which the desires harm the soul is by making it weak and tepid, so that it has no longer the strength to follow the path of virtue and to persevere in it. The philosophers tell us that virtue when it is collected in unity is stronger than when it is dispersed. It is clear, therefore, that, if the desire of the will is scattered among things other than virtue, it is of necessity so much weaker in the exercise of virtue. As hot water that is not covered soon begins to cool, and as aromatic spices that are not carefully wrapped gradually lose the strength of their fragrance, so the soul which is not collected in its singular desire for God loses the glow and vigor of its virtue. The desires which are not subdued will then grow and acquire such strength that they will eventually kill the soul's God-relationship because the soul has not first killed these desires.

CHAPTER XI

The will of the soul is to become one with the will of God.

Now it will be said that it is onerous and most difficult for the soul to attain to such purity and detachment that it has no desire and affection for anything. To this I reply: First, it is true that not all desires are equally harmful, nor do they equally encumber the soul (I am speaking of voluntary desires). For the natural desires place little or no obstacle in the way of the soul's union with God, as long as the soul does not give its consent and as long as these desires do not pass beyond the first movements. I have in mind all those desires in which the rational will has no part, either initially or afterward. For to free oneself of these—that is, to silence them completely in this life—is impossible. They may well be present in the natural part of man, and yet the rational spirit may be quite free from them. For it may sometimes happen that the soul abides in its will in the lofty union of the prayer of quietude, while these desires are actually present in the sensual part of man; in this case the higher part, which is in the state of prayer, will have no share in them. Yet all the other voluntary desires—whether they be of the nature of mortal sin (which are the gravest), or of the nature of venial sin (which are less grave), or whether they be only of the nature of imperfections (which are the least grave)—must be cast away. The soul must be free from them all, however small they be, if it is to arrive at this perfect union. The reason for this is that in the state of this Divine union the will of the soul is to be totally transformed into the will of God, so that there remains nothing in the soul that is contrary to the will of God and that, all in all, the movement of the soul completely coincides with the will of God.

This is why we say that in this state of union two wills become one, namely, the will of God, so that the will of God becomes the will of the soul. It is clear, then, that if the soul is to unite itself perfectly with God in love and will, it must first be free from all desire of [its own] will, however small. That is, the soul must not intentionally and knowingly consent with its will to any imperfection. I say "knowingly," because, unintentionally and unknowingly it may well fall into imperfections and venial sins; for of such non-voluntary sins it is written that the just man will fall seven times a day and will rise again. But as to voluntary desires, any one that is not overcome suffices to impede this Divine union.

Souls [which have not overcome such desires and attachments] not only make no progress but they even go backward, losing what they have gained on their way at the cost of so much time and labor. For it is well known that, on this road, not to go forward is to slide backward, and not to gain means to lose. Our Lord wanted to make us understand this when He said: "He who is not with Me, is against Me; and he who does not gather with Me, scatters" (Matt. 12:30). One imperfection is sufficient to lead to another, and these lead to yet more. The soul, after all, has only one will, and if this will is encumbered by anything or attached to anything, it is not free and pure, as is necessary for this Divine transformation.

If, then, one is to enter into this Divine union, all that lives in the soul of such a person must die, whether it be little or much, small or great, and the soul must remain without desire for all this and so thoroughly detached from it as though all these things were non-existent for the soul. This doctrine is clearly taught by St. Paul in his Epistle to the Corinthians, where he tells us: "I say to you, brethren, that the time is short; what remains for you and behoves you is that those who have wives should behave as though they had them not; that those who weep for the things of this world should act as though they wept not; and those who rejoice, as though they rejoiced not; and those who buy, as though they possessed nothing; and those who make use of the things of this world, as though they used them not" (1 Cor. 7:29-31).

CHAPTER XII

Voluntary and involuntary desires; mortal and venial sin.

We might well write at much greater length concerning this matter of the night of sense, but what has been said suffices for our purpose. It only remains, before we discuss the manner of entering into this night, to resolve a doubt which may have occurred to the reader.

It may be asked, first of all, if any desire suffices to work and cause in the soul the two evils of which we have spoken, namely, the privative or negative, which deprives the soul of the grace of God, and the positive, which causes in the soul the five major ills which we have described. Secondly, it may be asked if any desire, however small and of whatever kind, suffices to cause all these five together, or if some desires cause some and other desires cause others, some causing torment, others weariness, others darkness, and so on.

In answer to this, I say, first, that with respect to the privative evil, which deprives the soul of God, this is brought about wholly and exclusively only by voluntary desires which are of the nature of mortal sins; for they deprive the soul of grace in this life and of glory or the possession of God, in the life to come. And I say, secondly, that the desires which are of the nature of mortal sin as well as those voluntary desires which are of the nature of venial sin, and also those which are of the nature of imperfection, are each sufficient to cause in the soul all these positive evils together. And although these evils are in a certain sense privative, we call them here positive, since they are indicative of the soul's turning toward the creature, even as the privative evils are indicative of the soul's turning away from God. Yet there is this difference: whereas the desires that are of the nature of mortal sin cause total blindness, torment, impurity, weakness, and so on, those that are of the nature of venial sin or of imperfection do not produce these evils in their fullness or in the highest degree, since they do not deprive the soul of grace. That desire, then, which most weakens grace, will cause the most intense torment, the darkest blindness, and the greatest defilement.

The reason why any act of voluntary desire produces in the soul all these effects lies in the fact that such acts are diametrically opposed to all the acts of virtue, which produce the contrary effects in the soul. Just as an act of virtue produces or creates in the soul sweetness, peace, consolation, light, purity, and fortitude, so an inordinate desire causes torment, weariness, exhaustion, blindness, and weakness. All the virtues grow by the practice of any one of them, and so also all the vices increase by the practice of any one of them. And although all these evils are not visible at the time when the desire is indulged, since the concomitant pleasure does not allow it, yet sooner or later the evil effects are clearly seen. The truth of this can easily be confirmed

by those who allow themselves to be carried away by their
desires. Yet I know that some persons are too blind and
insensitive to feel this; for, as they do not walk in the ways
of God, they are unable to see what keeps them separated
from Him.

CHAPTER XIII

The active and the passive way; the imitation of Christ.

The soul usually enters into this night of sense in two ways:
the one is active; the other passive. By the active way we
mean whatever the soul can do and actually does by itself
in order to enter into this night. And we call passive the
mode in which the soul does nothing, in which it remains,
as it were, in a state of passivity, allowing God to work
in it. Of this we shall treat in the *fourth book.*

The counsels for the conquering of the desires, which
now follow, though brief and few in number, I believe to
be as helpful and efficacious as they are concise. He who
earnestly wishes to make practical use of them will need no
others, for he will find them all implied therein.

First, he should have an habitual inclination to imitate
Christ in everything he does, trying to conform himself to
His life. Let him meditate on the life of Christ, so that he
may learn how to imitate it and to behave in all things as
Christ would behave.

Secondly, to be able to do this well, every pleasure that
presents itself to the senses, if it be not purely for the honor
and glory of God, must be renounced; he must cast it out
for the love of Christ, Who in this life had and desired no
other pleasure than to do the will of His Father.

Let me give you the following example: If a person
were offered the pleasure of listening to things which are of

no value for the service and honor of God, he must neither
desire this pleasure nor desire to hear of these things; and
if he were offered the pleasure of looking at things which
do not help him on his journey toward God, he must not
desire this pleasure nor look at such things. And he should
behave in like manner with respect to all the senses. If this
is beyond his power, it suffices that he desire not to have
this pleasure whenever his sensory perception encounters
these things. In this manner he will succeed in depriving and
emptying his senses of all such pleasure, leaving them, as it
were, in darkness. In carefully following this counsel, he
will soon make much progress.

The silencing of the passions.

To silence and tranquillize the four natural passions—
joy, hope, fear, and grief—the following counsels are very
helpful, conducive to great merit, and the source of great
virtues:

Take care that you always choose
  Not the easiest, but the hardest;
  Not the most delectable, but the most distasteful;
  Not what gives most pleasure, but what is less pleas-
    ing;
  Not what allows you much rest, but what requires
    great exertion;
  Not what consoles, but what deprives you of con-
    solation;
  Not the loftiest and the most precious, but the lowest
    and the most despised;
  Not the desire for anything, but a desire for nothing.
  Do not go about seeking the best of temporal things,
    but the worst.
  Desire nothing but to enter for Christ's sake into
    total nakedness, emptiness, and poverty with re-
    spect to all the things of this world.

These counsels, if well heeded and put into practice, are quite sufficient for entering into the night of sense.

"Todo y nada": All and nothing.

In concluding this enumeration of counsels and rules, it is fitting to set down here those lines which are inscribed in the drawing at the beginning of this book, depicting the Ascent of the Mount [of Perfection]; they are instructions intended to teach the manner of ascending and thus attaining to the height of Divine union.

These lines read as follows:

If you want to have pleasure in everything,
    You must desire to have pleasure in nothing.

If you want to possess everything,
    You must desire to possess nothing.

If you want to become all,
    You must desire to be nothing.

If you want to know all,
    You must desire to know nothing.

If you want to arrive at that which you know not,
    You must go by a way which you know not.

If you want to arrive at that which you possess not,
    You must go by a way which you possess not.

If you want to arrive at that which you are not,
    You must pass through that which you are not.

The way not to obstruct the efficacy of the All.

If you allow yourself to be detained by anything,
    You desist from casting yourself upon the All.

For, in order to proceed from all things to the All,
    You must deny yourself wholly in all things.

If you are to attain to the possession of All,
    You must learn to possess it without desiring any-
        thing.

For, if you desire to possess anything at all,
    You cannot have your treasure in God alone.

In this nakedness the spiritual soul finds its quietude and rest; since it covets nothing, nothing wearies it in its upward flight, and nothing oppresses it when it is cast down; for the soul then abides in the center of its humility.

CHAPTER XIV

Explanation of the second line of the stanza.

"My longing heart aglow with love."

The soul, then, says that, "aglow with love in longing," it passed through the dark night of sense and attained to the union with its Beloved. For, in order to conquer all the desires and to deny itself those pleasures in all things with which its love and affection commonly enkindle the will, the soul must be set on fire by another and better love, which is the love of its Spouse. Having its pleasure and finding its strength in Him, the soul should then have the necessary courage and perseverance to deny itself all other things without too much effort. For it is a fact that the sensual nature is moved and attracted to the objects of sense with such yearnings of desire that, if the spiritual part [of the soul] is not set on fire by another and greater longing for the things of the spirit, the soul will be unable to throw off the yoke of nature or to enter into this night of sense.

CHAPTER XV

*The three remaining lines of the stanza: the liberation
of the soul.*

"Oh, blessed lot!—
I went forth unseen,
From my house that was at last in deepest rest."

These lines describe in a metaphorical manner the miserable state of the soul's captivity. He who is delivered from
this captivity, without being impeded by the jailers, considers this a "blessed lot." For the soul, owing to original
sin, is truly like a prisoner in this mortal body, subject to
natural passions and desires; and the soul calls it a "blessed
lot" to have escaped "unseen" from the fetters of its prison,
without being impeded by any of these passions and desires.
And the phrase, "my house lying at last in deepest rest,"
refers to the sensual part [of the soul], which houses all the
desires and which is now at rest because all these desires
have been overcome and put to sleep. For the soul does not
attain to true freedom in the fruition of its union with its
Beloved until the desires are put to sleep by the mortification of the senses and until the senses themselves are thus
no longer stirred by desire and can no longer wage war
against the spirit.

BOOK TWO

The First Dark Night of the Spirit: Faith

CHAPTER I

Exposition of the second stanza.

Secure—protected by darkness,
I climbed the secret ladder, in disguise,
—Oh, blessed lot!—
In darkness, veiled and concealed, I went,
Leaving behind my house in deepest rest.

In this second stanza the soul sings of the blessed venture it embarked on when it stripped the spirit of all spiritual imperfections and of all desire for the possession of the things of the spirit. This is for the soul a much greater venture because of the fact that it is much more difficult to put to rest this house of the soul's spiritual part, to enter into the interior darkness of spiritual detachment from all things —both sensual and spiritual—and to ascend to God, leaning on pure faith alone. The soul here speaks of a "secret ladder," because all the steps and parts of this ladder are totally hidden from both sense and understanding, so that the soul is left in darkness with respect to all the (natural) light of sense and understanding. It goes forth, passing beyond all the limits of nature and reason, in order to ascend by this Divine ladder of faith, which leads and penetrates to the innermost Being of God. And the soul says that it was going forth "in disguise," because, as it ascends by faith, its garments or its natural condition are being divinized. And this disguise was the cause of its not being recognized or detained, neither by temporal things, nor by things of a rational nature, nor by Satan; for none of these things can harm a soul that travels on the road of faith. Such a soul walks truly "in darkness and in concealment," that is to say, hidden from the eyes of Satan, to whom the light of faith is darker than any darkness.

The soul says furthermore that it passed through this spiritual night, "leaving behind its house in deepest rest," which means that its spiritual and rational part was at rest. When, therefore, the soul attains to union with God, it has put to rest not only its natural powers or faculties but also the impulses and anxious desires of its spiritual part. For, in order to put to rest the house of the spirit, all that is needed is a denial of all the spiritual faculties, pleasures, and appetites, in the purity of faith. Once this is accomplished, the soul is united with its Beloved in a union of simplicity, purity, love, and similitude.

While in the night of sense there still remains some light—since there remain understanding and reason, which are not blinded—this spiritual night of faith deprived the soul of everything pertaining to understanding and sense. And this is why the soul in this night says that it was travelling "securely and protected by darkness." For however little the soul may work [in this night] by its own power, it walks more securely, because it walks more in faith.

CHAPTER II

The night of faith blinds the light of reason.

What now follows, describes the second part of this night, which is *faith*. As we have said, faith is the marvellous means which leads us to the end that is God, Who is also to the soul a third cause (or the third part) of this night. For faith, as a means [leading toward the end], is comparable to midnight; and we may say that [this second part of the dark night] is darker to the soul than the first part and, in a way, darker also than the third part. Though it is true that God is as dark a night to the soul as is faith, nonetheless, when the three parts of the night are over, God begins to illumine the soul in a supernatural manner with the rays of His Divine light. And this light is the beginning of the perfect union that follows upon the passing of the third night; wherefore the latter may be said to be less dark.

Faith is also darker than the first part [of this night], for the first part pertains to the lower or sensual part of man and is therefore more exterior; whereas the second part of this night—that is, faith—pertains to the higher or rational part of man and is more interior and more obscure, since it deprives [the soul] of the light of reason, or, to say it more precisely, faith blinds the light of reason. This second part of the dark night [namely, faith] may thus well be compared to midnight, which is deepest and darkest night.

CHAPTER III

"Faith comes from hearing" (Rom: 10:17).

The theologians call faith a habit of the soul, and they add that faith is both certain and obscure. They call it an obscure habit because it makes us believe truths revealed by God Himself, truths which transcend all natural light and are beyond all human understanding. And this is why this superabundant light that is given to the soul in faith is blackest darkness: it does away with things great and small, even as the light of the sun outshines all other lights to such an extent that when it shines and overwhelms our power of vision these minor lights seem no longer to be lights at all. In a similar manner the light of faith, by its surpassing brilliance, overwhelms and eclipses the light of the understanding, which, of its own power, extends only to natural knowledge, notwithstanding the fact that the understanding has a receptive faculty for the supernatural which is acti-

vated whenever it pleases Our Lord to dispose it to supernatural action.

Faith tells us of things which we have never either seen
or understood, neither as they are in themselves nor in any
similitude, since there is nothing that resembles them. And
thus we have no light of natural knowledge that could illuminate the things of faith, since what we are told of them
has no proportionate relationship to any of our senses. For,
as St. Paul says, "Faith comes from hearing" (Rom. 10:17),
by which he means that faith is not a knowledge that enters
by way of any of the senses; it is rather the consent given
by the soul to that which it has been told.

Whereas other kinds of knowledge and science can be
acquired by the [natural] light of the understanding, the
science and knowledge of faith is acquired without this light;
the light of the understanding is even extinguished, so that
the soul may be illumined by the greater light of faith. This
is why Isaiah said: "Unless you believe, you shall not understand" (Is. 7:9). It is clear, then, that faith is indeed a dark
night to the soul, and, as such, it imparts light to the soul:
the deeper the soul is in the darkness of faith, the more it
is illumined; for it is by blinding that faith gives light. Thus
the saying of David, "The night will illumine me in my delights," means that in the delights of pure contemplation
and union with God, faith will be his guide. And he wants
it to be understood that the soul must be in darkness in
order to have light on this road.

CHAPTER IV

To be guided by faith, the soul must be in darkness.

It seems to be appropriate at this juncture to describe in
greater detail the darkness that must be in the soul if it
wishes to enter into this abyss of faith. If a soul aspires to
supernatural transformation, it is clear that it must be far

removed from all that is contained in its sensual and rational nature. For we call supernatural that which transcends nature, so that the natural is left behind. The soul must completely and by its own will empty itself of everything that can be contained in it with respect to affection and volition, in such a way that, regardless of how many supernatural gifts it may receive, it will remain detached from them and in darkness. It must be like a blind man, finding its only support in dark faith, taking it as its guide and light, and leaning upon none of the things which it understands, enjoys, feels, and imagines. And if the soul does not make itself blind in this manner, remaining in total darkness, it will not attain to those greater things which are taught by faith.

When St. Paul said: "He who would come into the presence of God, must first believe that God exists" (Heb. 11:6), he meant by this that he who aspires to being joined with God in perfect union must not walk by the way of understanding, nor lean on either joyful sensations, or inner feelings, or imagination, but he must believe in God's Being, which is hidden as much from the understanding as from desire, imagination and any other sensory apperception, nor can it be known at all in this life in its essential nature. Even the highest concerning God that can be felt and perceived in this life is infinitely remote from Him and from the pure possession of Him. The goal which the soul pursues is thus beyond even the highest things that can be known or perceived. And the soul must therefore pass beyond everything to a state of unknowing.

The soul which attains to this state makes no longer use of any particular ways or methods—whether they relate to understanding, apperception, or feeling—although it bears within itself all possible ways, after the manner of one who owns nothing, yet possesses all things.

On this road, then, the soul, by becoming blind in its faculties, will see the light, as Our Saviour says in the Gospel: "I have come into this world for judgment, that those who are blind should see, and those who see should become blind" (John 9:39). This saying evidently applies to this spiritual road, where the soul which has entered into darkness and has become blind in all its natural lights, will learn to see supernaturally.

And in order that we may proceed from here on with less confusion, it appears necessary to describe in the following chapter what we mean when we speak of the union of the soul with God. For, once this is clearly understood, what we shall have to say in subsequent chapters will become a great deal more intelligible.

CHAPTER V

*The union of the soul with God is a union of love
and of likeness, not division of substance.*

To understand, then, the nature of this union, it must be known that God dwells or is present substantially [*per essentiam*] in every soul, even in the soul of the greatest sinner. This kind of union between God and all His creatures is never lacking, since it is in and by this union that He sustains their being; and if it were ever lacking, these creatures would immediately cease to be and would fall back into nothingness. Thus, if we here speak of the union of the soul with God, we do not have in mind this ever-present substantial union, but we do mean that union of the soul with God which is consummated in the soul's transformation in God—a union which can come about only when the soul attains to a likeness with God by virtue of love. We shall therefore call this the union of likeness, to distinguish it from the union of substance or essence. The former is supernatural, the latter natural. And the supernatural union comes about when the two wills—that of the soul and that of God—are conformed in one, so that there is nothing in the one that is repugnant to the other. Thus, when the soul rids itself totally of that which is repugnant

to and not in conformity with the Divine will, it is transformed in God through love.

This applies not only to whatever is repugnant to God
in human action, but also in habit, so that the soul must not
only desist from all voluntary acts of imperfection but must
also completely overcome the acquired habits of these imperfections. And since no creature nor the actions or capa-
bilities of any creature can ever measure up or attain to
that which is God, the soul must be stripped of all creaturely attachments as well as of its own activities and capa-
bilities—that is to say, of its understanding, its likings, and
its feelings—so that, when all that which is unlike God and
unconformed to Him is cast out, the soul may then receive
the likeness of God.

Supernatural being is communicated only by love and
grace. Not all souls, however, abide in God's love and grace,
and those who do abide in them do not possess them in the
same degree; for some attain higher degrees of love than
others. And thus, God communicates Himself most to that
soul which has progressed farthest in love and has most
conformed its will to God's will. And that soul which has
attained to a total conformity and likeness of its will and
God's will is totally united with Him and supernaturally
transformed in Him.

Let me clarify [the nature of this union] by a simile.
Picture a ray of sunlight that is striking a window. Now
if the window is coated with stains or vapors, the ray will
be unable to illumine it and transform it into its own light;
this it could do only if the window were stainless and pure.
And the greater or lesser degree of illumination will be
strictly in proportion to the window's greater or lesser purity;
and this will be so, not because of the ray of sunlight but
because of the condition of the window. Thus, if the window were entirely clean and pure, the ray would transform
and illumine it in such a way that it would become almost
undistinguishable from the brightness of the ray and would
diffuse the same light as the ray. And yet, however much

the window may resemble the ray of sunlight, it actually retains its own distinct nature. But this does not prevent us from saying that this window is luminous as a ray of the sun or is sunlight by participation. Now the soul is like this window: the Divine light of the Being of God is unceasingly beating upon it, or, to use a better expression, the Divine light is ever dwelling in it.

When the soul thus allows God to work in it, it will soon be transformed and transfigured in God, and God will communicate to it His supernatural Being in such a way that the soul appears to be God Himself, and it will indeed be God by participation. Yet it remains true nevertheless that the soul's natural being—notwithstanding the soul's supernatural transformation—remains as distinct from the Being of God as it was before, even as the window has and retains a nature of its own, distinct from the nature of the ray, although it owes its luminosity to the light of the sun.

This consideration should make it clearer why a soul can not dispose itself for this union by either understanding, or sensory apperception, or inner feelings and imaginings, or by any other experiences relating either to God or to anything else, but only by purity and love, that is, by perfect resignation and total detachment from all things for the sake of God alone. And as there can be no perfect transformation unless there be perfect purity, the soul will not be perfect unless it be totally cleansed and wholly pure.

Those souls [who attain to Divine union] do so according to their greater or smaller capacity and thus not in the same degree; and the degree of union depends also on what the Lord wishes to grant to each soul. And it is similar in the beatific vision: though some souls will have a more perfect vision of God in Heaven than others, they all see God, and all are content, since their capacity is satisfied. And in this life, too, all souls [who have attained to the state of perfection] will be equally satisfied, each one according to its knowledge of God and thus according to its capacity. A soul, on the other hand, that does not attain to a degree of purity corresponding to its capacity, will never find true peace and contentment.

CHAPTER VI

The three theological virtues perfect the three faculties of the soul.

We shall now endeavor to show how the three faculties of the soul—understanding, memory, and will—are brought into this spiritual night, which is the means leading to the end of Divine union. To do this, it is necessary first of all to explain in this chapter how the three theological virtues—faith, hope, and love [*caritas*]—by means of which the soul is united with God according to its faculties, produce an identical emptiness and darkness, each one with respect to its corresponding faculty. Thus, faith produces darkness in the understanding; hope, in the memory; love, in the will. Subsequently, we shall describe how the understanding is perfected in the darkness of faith, and memory in the emptiness of hope; and we shall then show how the will must be voided and stripped of all affection in order to move toward God. For, as we have pointed out, the soul is united with God in this life not through the understanding, nor through joyous feelings, nor through imagination, nor through any other sensory experience; but only through faith, which perfects the understanding; through hope, which perfects the memory; and through love, which perfects the will.

Faith, then, tells us what cannot be comprehended with the [natural] *understanding.* According to St. Paul, "Faith is the substance of our hopes; it convinces us of things we cannot see" (Heb. 11:1). Although the understanding may give its consent with a firm and perfect assurance, the things of faith are not revealed to the understanding; for, if they were revealed to it, there would be no need for faith. Wherefore, though faith gives certainty to the understanding, it does not illumine it, but leaves it in darkness.

As to *hope,* there is no doubt that it in its turn plunges the *memory* into emptiness and darkness with respect to both things here below and things above. For hope has always to do with that which is not yet in our possession, since, if we already possessed it, there would no longer be room for hope. This is what St. Paul means when he says: "Hope would no longer be hope if its object were in plain view; for how could a man still hope for something that is fully seen [that is, fully possessed]?" (Rom. 8:24).

And, similarly, *love* empties the *will* of all things, since it obliges us to love God above them all; this, however, we cannot do unless we detach our affection from all of them in order to attach it wholly to God. Wherefore, Christ tells us through the mouth of St. Luke: "No one can be My disciple who does not detach himself from all that he [wilfully] possesses" (Luke, 14:33). All three of these virtues, then, plunge the soul into darkness and emptiness with respect to all things.

This, then, is the spiritual night which we have called *active;* for all the soul is able to do to enter into this night, it does by its own power. And as, when we were speaking of the night of sense, we described a method of emptying the faculties of sense of all the objects of sense—so that the soul might advance from its point of departure to the intermediate state of faith—so also, in this spiritual night, we shall, with Divine aid, describe a method whereby the spiritual faculties are emptied and purified of all that is not God. As a result, the spiritual faculties will then be placed in the darkness of the three [theological] virtues, which, as we have seen, are the means that dispose the soul for its union with God. And it should be noted that I am now speaking in particular to those who have begun to enter the state of contemplation.

CHAPTER VII

The narrow road; detachment of the understanding; spiritual poverty.

Speaking of the road [that leads to eternal life], Our Saviour said: "How small is the the gate and how narrow the road that leads to Life; and there are few who find it" (Matt. 7:14). Now what Christ says of the small gate, we may understand in relation to the sensual part of man; and what He says of the narrow road, may be understood in relation to the spiritual or rational part. And the reason for His saying that "there are few who find it" is that there are few who know how to enter and who actually desire to enter into this total nakedness and emptiness of the spirit. For this path that leads to the high mountain of perfection is steep and narrow and therefore requires travellers who are not weighed down and encumbered by any cares for either the lower things of sense or the higher things of the spirit. Since this is an undertaking in which the prize of our search is God alone, He alone must be the object of our striving and our victory.

Hence we can see clearly that the soul which travels on this road must not only be free from all creaturely attachments but must also be spiritually poor and as dead to its own self. This is why Our Lord taught us through the mouth of St. Mark that priceless doctrine which, because of its great importance and because it specifically applies to our purpose, I shall quote here in full and then explain in its true spiritual meaning.

Our Lord says: "If any man wishes to go My way, let him deny his own self, and take up his cross, and follow Me. He who tries to save his life will lose it; but he who loses his life for My sake will save it" (Mark 8:34-35).

I wish someone would properly teach us how to understand, practise, and inwardly grasp the true meaning and significance of this counsel, so that spiritual persons would see how different is the method they should employ on this road from what many of them regard as proper. While some believe that any kind of withdrawal from the world and any external reform suffice, others are content with practising the virtues and continuing in prayer and penance; but neither attain to that nakedness, self-denial, and spiritual poverty which the Lord here commends to us; for they prefer feeding and clothing their natural selves with spiritual feelings and consolations to emptying themselves of all things and renouncing their natural selves for God's sake. Or they think that it suffices to strip their natural selves of worldly things, without purifying themselves by the total renunciation also of spiritual attachments. Thus, when they get a glimpse of this concrete and perfect life of the spirit—which manifests itself in the complete absence of all sweetness, in aridity, distaste, and in the many trials that are the true spiritual cross—they flee from it as from death. What they seek in their communion with God is sweet and delectable feelings; but this is a sort of spiritual gluttony rather than self-denial and spiritual poverty. As far as their spirituality is concerned, they become enemies of Christ. They seek themselves in God, which is the very opposite of love; for to seek oneself in God is to seek the favors and refreshing delights of God, whereas to seek God in oneself is to incline oneself to choose, for Christ's sake, all that is most distasteful; and this is love of God.

And when Our Lord said that he who tries to save his life will lose it, He meant that he who desires to possess anything for himself will lose it; whereas he who for Christ's sake renounces all that his will can desire and enjoy, and chooses that which is most like to the Cross, will save his life. This is precisely what His Majesty taught to those two disciples [the sons of Zebedee] who asked that they be allowed a place on His right and on His left. He answered their request for such glory by offering them the cup of which He had to drink, as a thing more precious and more secure on this earth than any joy of possession.

To drink of this cup, however, is to die to the natural self by detachment and self-annihilation, so that the soul may be able to travel by this narrow path unimpeded, since there remains to it nothing but self-denial and the Cross. And this Cross is the pilgrim's staff on which the soul may lean on its way to God and which greatly eases its burden and travail. Wherefore Our Lord said through the mouth of St. Matthew: "My yoke is easy, and My burden is light" (Matt. 11:30). For if a man resolves to carry this cross willingly, that is, if he is truly determined to undergo and bear hardships and trials for God's sake, he will find in them great solace and sweetness. If, on the other hand, he desires to possess anything or remains attached to anything whatsoever, his self is not totally stripped and emptied of all things, and he will not be able to continue his upward journey on this narrow path. For progress [in the spiritual life] can be made only by imitating Christ, Who is the Way, the Truth, and the Life; and no one can come to the Father, except through Christ (cf. John 14:6).

Christ, then, is the Way, and this way is death to the natural self in both sense and spirit. And I shall now try to explain how we must die [to our natural selves], following the example of Christ, Who is our guiding light.

First, it is certain that, as far as the senses are concerned, He died (spiritually) in His life and (naturally) in His death. For, as He said, He had not in His life where to lay His head, and in His death He had even less.

Second, it is equally certain that in the hour of His death He felt annihilated and abandoned also in His soul, deprived of all consolation and help, since His Father left His humanity in a state of such complete aridity that the cry "My God, My God, why hast Thou forsaken Me?" (Matt. 27:46) forced itself upon His lips. This was, with respect to His sensory nature, the greatest desolation He had suffered in His life. And yet, it was then that he wrought the greatest work of His entire life, greater than any of His miracles and other mighty deeds—the reconciliation and union of the human race with God, through grace.

The words of David, "I was reduced to nothingness and unknowing," (Ps. 72:22), point to the mystery of the small gate and the narrow way, so that the truly spiritual man may learn to understand the way of Christ, the way of union with God. He will learn from these words that the more he becomes as nothing, the more intimately he is united with God and the greater is the work that he accomplishes. This union, then, consists not in delights, consolations, and sweet spiritual feelings, but in a living sensual and spiritual, internal and external, death of the cross.

CHAPTER VIII

No creature nor any knowledge that can be comprehended by the understanding can serve as proximate means of union with God.

Before we enter into a discussion of faith—the appropriate means of union with God—it seems necessary to demonstrate that no created thing, whether it be real or a product of our imagination, can serve the understanding as a proper means of union with God; and that everything that falls within the reach of the understanding is an impediment rather than a means, if the understanding desires to cling to it. In this present chapter we are offering a general demonstration, but subsequently we shall discuss this matter in greater detail.

It is one of the principal rules of philosophy that all means must be proportioned to the end; that is, they must have some proportionate relation to and some similarity with the end. If, for example, fire is to be joined with wood, it is necessary that heat, which is the means, first prepare the wood, by transmitting to it such an intensity of heat that the wood will acquire a high degree of similarity or a proportionate assimilation to fire. Similarly, if the understanding is to be united with God—as far as this is possible in this life—it is necessary that the understanding employ that means which bears the closest resemblance to Him.

Here it should be pointed out that no creature—high or low—approximates God or bears any resemblance to His Being. For, though it is true that all creatures have, as the theologians tell us, a certain relation to God and bear a Divine impress—some more and others less, according to the greater or lesser amount of being of their natures—yet there is no essential similarity between them and God. On the contrary, the distance between their being and His Divine Being is infinite. And therefore it is impossible for the understanding to attain to God by means of creatures—whether they be celestial or earthly—since there is no proportionate similitude between God and creatures. No creature, then, can serve the understanding as a proportionate means to attain to God. Nor can anything that the imagination is able to imagine or that the understanding is capable of receiving and comprehending in this life be a proximate means of union with God. Neither can the understanding with its insight comprehend anything that is like Him, nor can the will taste any delight and sweetness comparable to that which is God, nor can the memory inject into the imagination any representations and images that mirror Him. It is clear, then, that none of these kinds of knowledge can lead the understanding straightway to God. In order to reach Him, the soul must go forward by not-understanding rather than by desiring to understand, by rendering itself blind and by entering into darkness rather than by opening its eyes.

Contemplation is a secret wisdom concerning God and is therefore called mystical theology.

And thus *contemplation*—by which the understanding is given the most sublime knowledge of God—is called *mystical theology,* because it is a secret wisdom concerning

God: it is a secret even to the very understanding that receives it. And this is why Dionysius [the Areopagite] calls this wisdom a ray of darkness. Aristotle tells us that, as the eyes of the bat are in total darkness with respect to the sun, so is our understanding in total darkness to that which is brightest in God. And he adds that the more sublime and luminous the things of God are in themselves, the more obscure and unknown they are to us. And the Apostle Paul confirms this when he says: The most sublime things of God are the least known to men.

CHAPTER IX

Faith is the proximate and proportionate means to ascend to the Divine union of love.

Faith alone, then, is the proximate and proportionate means that leads the soul to union with God. For the likeness between faith and God is so great that the only remaining difference is that between believing in God and seeing Him. God is infinite, and faith presents Him to us as infinite; God is Three-and-One, and faith presents Him to us as Three-and-One; God is darkness to our understanding, and faith likewise blinds and dazzles our understanding. By this means alone, then, God manifests Himself to the soul in a Divine light that surpasses all understanding. And therefore, the greater the faith of the soul, the more it is united with God.

Whensoever God revealed Himself in loving communication, He manifested Himself in darkness; as may, for example, be seen in the case of Job, of whom it is said in Scripture that God spoke with him from the air in darkness (Job 38:1; and 40:1). This darkness signifies the obscurity of faith wherein the Godhead is concealed when It communicates Itself to the soul. And this darkness will be no more when, as St. Paul says, that which is imperfect—that is, the darkness of faith—shall end, and the perfect fulfillment —that is, the Divine light—will have come.

CHAPTER X

The different types and modes of knowledge that can be comprehended by the understanding: natural and supernatural knowledge.

In order to be able to discuss in detail the gain and loss which may be caused in the soul—in regard to faith as the means to attain to Divine union—by the notions and apprehensions of the understanding, it is necessary here to make a distinction between the different kinds of apprehensions which the soul may receive, whether they be natural or supernatural.

We must know, then, that the understanding can receive intellectual knowledge in two ways, the one natural, the other supernatural. The natural way comprises all that the understanding can understand, whether by means of the bodily senses or by its own [natural] power. The supernatural way comprises all that is given to the understanding above and beyond its natural capacity and ability.

Among the different kinds of supernatural knowledge, some are of a corporeal and some of a spiritual nature. The former are two in number: some are received by way of the external bodily senses, others by way of the internal bodily senses, and therein is included all that the imagination can apprehend, conceive, or fabricate. And spiritual supernatural knowledge is also of two kinds: some of it is clear and distinct, and some of it is confused, indefinite, and obscure. Among the clear and distinct kinds [of supernatural knowledge] there are four classes of apprehensions which are communicated to the spirit without the intermediary of any bodily sense: they are visions, [private] revela-

tions, locutions, and spiritual feelings. The obscure and indefinite type [of supernatural knowledge] is of one kind only:
this is *contemplation,* which is given [to the soul] in faith;
and this is the end to which we have to lead the soul by way
of all these means.

CHAPTER XI

*The hindrance and harm that may be caused
by supernatural experiences.*

What we have to discuss in this chapter concerns those kinds
of knowledge and those apprehensions which pertain exclusively to the supernatural understanding and which come
to it by way of the external bodily senses, that is, by seeing,
hearing, smelling, tasting, and touching. With respect to
sight, spiritual persons not infrequently are experiencing the
presence of forms and figures that are representations of
persons from the life beyond, such as apparitions of certain
saints, of angels and demons, or certain phenomena of light
of extraordinary splendor. Or they may hear certain unfamiliar words, sometimes spoken by these appearances, and
sometimes without their being able to see the person who
speaks. As to the sense of smell, they may have a sensory
experience of the sweetest fragrance, without their being
able to recognize its source and cause. And, likewise, with
respect to taste and touch, they may sense at times the
sweetest savours and experience great delight, to such a degree that it is as though all their bones and marrow were
rejoicing in jubilation and as though they were bathed in
joyous rapture. This experience bears a certain resemblance
to what is known as spiritual unction, which in pure souls
issues from the spirit and flows into the very members of
the body. And this experience of sweetness in sensory perception is a fairly common thing with spiritual persons, for

it results from the spiritual quality of their sensible affection and devotion.

Now it should be remembered that, though all these things may be experienced by the bodily senses in the way of God's dispensation, our senses must never rely on these experiences or permit them to enter [the soul], but must rather resolutely turn away from them, without even trying to determine whether they are good or evil; for, the more external and corporeal they are, the less certainty there is that they are worked by God, since God ordinarily and preferably communicates Himself to the spirit—wherein there is more security and benefit for the soul—rather than to sense, wherein there is usually much danger of deception. For the bodily senses are as ignorant of the things of the spirit as a brute is of rational things, and even more so.

He, then, who has a high regard for such sensed phenomena errs greatly and places himself in great danger of being deceived. To say the least, he will block his way to spirituality. For, as we have previously stated, there exists no proportionate relationship between all these corporeal things and the things of the spirit. And thus it may be assumed that such sensed phenomena are more likely to be worked by Satan than by God, since the devil wields more power and can deceive more easily in that which is external and corporeal than in that which is more internal and spiritual. Such representations and feelings should therefore always be rejected; for even if we grant that some of them may be worked by God, He is never offended if the soul rejects them and desires them not; nor is the soul on that account less assured of the good effect and fruit which God may wish to produce in the soul by means of these phenomena.

The reason for this is that if God produces any corporeal vision or any other sensory perception, or if He wishes to communicate Himself to the inwardness of the soul, the effect is felt in the spirit instantaneously, without

even giving the soul time to deliberate whether to accept
or reject such communication. For these things are worked
in the spirit *passively,* so that the will is not at liberty to
either seek them or reject them. It is as though a naked body
were exposed to fire: it would matter little whether or not
that person desired to be burned, since the fire would per-
force do its work. And it is the same with visions and representations that are good: they produce their effect in the
soul, whether the soul desires it or not. But those that are
worked by the devil—without the soul's desire and consent
—cause tumultuous unrest, or aridity, or vanity and spiritual
pride. Yet these latter effects are not as potent in working
evil as are those produced by God in working good; for
those produced by the devil can move the will only in-
directly, by giving rise to initial movements [in the senses
and in the imagination], unless the will gives its consent. And
the disquietude [thus engendered in the soul] is of short
duration, unless the soul's lack of fortitude and prudence
causes its prolongation.

The soul, then, should never be so presumptuous as to
desire such experiences, even though they be of God; for
if it desires to receive them, the following six kinds of impediments will ensue: First, faith becomes more and more
feeble; for the objects of the senses detract from faith, since
faith, as we have seen, transcends all sense experience. Thus,
if the soul does not close its eyes to all the objects of sense,
it withdraws itself from the proper means of union with
God [viz., faith]. Secondly, if these [objects of sense] are
not rejected, they impede the spirit; for the soul is then detained by them, and its spirituality cannot rise to the invisible. Thirdly, the soul becomes attached to these things
and does not advance to true resignation and spiritual detachment. Fourthly, the soul gradually loses the inward
spiritual effects which are caused by these things, because it
fixes its eyes on their sensual aspect, which is the least important. Fifthly, the soul begins to lose the favors of God,
because it appropriates these things possessively and thus

derives no real benefit from them. Sixthly, by its desire [for such experiences] the soul opens the door to the devil, making it easy for him to deceive it with phenomena of a similar appearance, so that they may assume the guise of good; for the devil is an expert in the arts of dissimulation and disguise and can, as St. Paul says, pose as an angel of light (2 Cor. 11:14).

If, however, the soul defeats the devil on the first step [of the spiritual way], it will pass on to the second; and if it does likewise on the second step, it will go on to the third; and thence onward through all the seven mansions—that is, the seven steps of love—until the Spouse shall take it into the cellar of wine of His perfect love.

Happy the soul that has learned how to fight against that beast of the Apocalypse (13:1), which has seven heads—the counterparts of the seven steps of love; and with its seven heads this beast wages war against the soul in each of the seven mansions, in which the soul strengthens itself by spiritual exercise as it ascends step by step to the [perfect] love of God. And there is no doubt that if the soul fights faithfully and victoriously against each of these heads, it will deserve to pass from one step to the next, and from mansion to mansion, until it reaches the last. So furious, however, is this war that, according to St. John (Apoc. 13:7), this beast "was allowed to wage war even upon the saints" and could triumph over them on each one of these steps of love.

It is therefore much to be lamented that many who engage in this battle against the beast do not even succeed in destroying its first head, by denying themselves the worldly objects of sense. And while some do succeed and do destroy this first head, they do not cut off the second, namely, the visions of sense. But the most deplorable thing of all is that some, after having destroyed not only the first and second but even the third head—that is, the internal senses—and after having left behind the state of meditation, are overcome by this spiritual beast at the very moment when they were about to enter into the purity of spirit. For at that moment the beast rises up against them once more, and even its first head comes to life again, so that in their falling back the last state of these souls is worse than the first, since the beast now brings along seven other spirits more wicked than itself (cf. Luke 11:26).

The spiritual person, then, has to deny himself all the apprehensions and temporal delights that pertain to the external senses, if he wants to destroy the first and the second head of this beast and enter in living faith into the first and second chamber of love.

CHAPTER XII

Natural imaginary apprehensions cannot be a proportionate means to attain to union with God.

What must first be discussed now is that internal bodily sense known as imagination and fancy. This internal sense must likewise be emptied of all those imaginative forms and apprehensions with which it may be naturally occupied; and we must show here how impossible it is for the soul to attain to union with God until it ceases to be actively preoccupied with them.

It must be known, then, that the sense of which we are here speaking in particular consists really of two internal bodily senses—imagination and fancy—which are subservient one to the other in due order. For the one thinks, as it were, by imagining, while the other uses the power of fancy to give form to the imagination (or to that which is imagined). All the things, then, which these senses can receive and construe are called imaginations and fantasies [or phantasms], that is, forms which are represented in these senses by means of corporeal images and figures. These can be of two kinds: they are supernatural if they can be and are represented in these senses *passively;* and these we call supernaturally induced imaginary visions. Others are natural, which means that the soul can produce them within itself *actively,* by its own operative ability, in the shape of forms, figures, and images. And thus to these two faculties pertains *meditation,* which is a discursive mental activity by means of images, forms, and figures that are produced imaginatively by these two senses; as happens, for example, when we picture in our imagination Christ crucified, or bound to the pillar, or at one of the other stations [of the Cross]. Or our imagination may envision God seated upon a throne with great majesty; or we may meditate imaginatively on the radiant beauty of the light of Glory, and so on. Now the soul must be emptied of all these imagined forms, figures, and images, and it must remain in darkness with respect to these [internal] senses if it is to attain to Divine union; for these [contents of the imagination] cannot serve as proportionate means of union with God any more than can the corporeal objects of the five external senses.

The reason of this is that the imagination cannot fashion or imagine anything beyond that which it has experienced by means of the external senses—that is, beyond that which it has seen with the eyes, heard with the ears, and so on. The most it can do is to compound likenesses of the things which it has seen, or heard, or felt; and these composites do not even possess as much substantial reality as the apprehensions that have been received by the external senses. For, though one may envision with the imagination palaces made of pearls and mountains of gold—because the sight of pearls and of gold is familiar to sense experience—all this is actually less than the essence of one small piece of gold or one single pearl, although to the imagination the composite appears greater in quantity and ideal splendor.

Those, therefore, who imagine they can find God beneath any of these figures, are very far indeed from approaching Him. For, though these forms and modes of meditation are necessary for beginners, so that by means of sensory perceptions they may feed and enkindle their souls with love—thus using them as remote means to union with God and spiritual repose—yet they must merely pass through them and never allow themselves to be detained by them. Just so the stairs of a staircase are merely the means to reach the top of the staircase and the room to which it leads. And if the person who climbs the stairs would want to stay on any one of them, he would never arrive at the top. Similarly, the soul which is to attain in this life to the union of that supreme repose and bliss must pass through and leave behind all the steps of these meditations, forms, and apprehensions; for they bear no resemblance or proportion to the goal to which they lead, which is God.

Many spiritual persons commit this grave error: they have started out—as it befits beginners—by trying to approach God by means of certain images, forms, and meditations; but now God wishes to use their collected spiritual strength to lead them further on to more spiritual—internal and invisible—treasures, by depriving them of all taste for the delights of discursive meditation; and they do not possess the required ability, courage, and knowledge that would enable them to detach themselves from those more tangible methods to which they have grown accustomed. And so they continually labor to retain them, finding, however, little or no sweetness in their efforts but rather experience an increasing aridity and weariness of soul. For, as we have pointed out, the soul enjoys no longer that food of sense but needs another kind of food, more delicate, more internal and less of the nature of sense, a food which imparts to the soul deep spiritual quietude and repose. And the more the soul learns to abide in the spiritual, the more comes to a halt the operation of its faculties in particular acts, since the soul becomes more and more collected in one undivided and pure act. And thus the faculties cease to work, even as the feet cease to move and come to a halt when the journey is ended. For if the movement of going were forever to continue, one would never arrive; and if there were nothing but end-less means, it is hard to see when and where there could ever be a fruition of the end and the goal.

As these souls, however, are unfamiliar with the mystery of this novel experience, they are apt to believe that they are idle and are doing nothing at all [in this state]; and they allow themselves no rest, but endeavor to continue their meditating and reasoning. The result is that they are filled with desolation and aridity, since they are trying to find sweetness where none can any longer be found. We may even say that the greater their endeavor, the smaller their progress, for the more they persist in the pursuit [of this method], the worse becomes their state of mind, because their soul is drawn farther and farther away from spiritual peace. By trying to retrace their steps and to do all over again what has already been done, they give up the greater for the less. To such persons, therefore, we must give the advice to learn how to abide in the quietude of the presence of God, attentively, patiently, and lovingly, paying no heed to the work of the imagination. For, as we have previously stated, here the faculties [of the soul] are at rest, or rather, they are working not actively, but passively, by receiving that which God works in them.

CHAPTER XIII

The signs whereby the spiritual person may know when to pass to the state of contemplation are (1) inability to meditate discursively; (2) inability to fix the imagination on particular objects; (3) concentration of attention on God.

Although it is quite proper for a spiritual person to lay aside [discursive imaginative meditation] in due time, it is nonetheless mandatory that he not give up this kind of meditation prematurely, lest he should turn backward. We shall therefore here set down certain signs and indications which the spiritual person will find in himself, whereby he may know whether or not the time has come [to pass from the state of meditation to the state of contemplation].

The first sign is an inner awareness that he is no longer able to meditate discursively and with the accustomed spiritual gain by way of the imagination; he rather finds now aridity in that which formerly used to attract his senses and bring him sweet delight. But as long as he finds delight in meditation and discursive reasoning, he should not abandon them, unless his soul has entered into that peace and quiet which are described below as the third sign.

The second sign is a realization that he has no longer any desire to fix his imagination or his senses on particular objects, whether they be external or internal.

The third and surest sign is that the soul delights in being alone, its loving attention being fixed upon God in inward peace, quietude, and rest, without engaging in any particular meditation and without positing acts and exercising the faculties of memory, understanding, and will—at least, without any discursive acts, that is, without passing from one thing to another.

These three signs at least the spiritual person must recognize in himself, and *in conjunction,* before he can safely venture to leave behind the state of meditation and sense, and enter the state of contemplation and spirit.

And it is not sufficient if the first sign is present without the second, for it may well be that the reason for a person's inability to use the imagination in meditating on the things of God is his distraction and indolence. Nor does it suffice that he observe in himself the first and second sign, if he does not observe, conjoined with these, the third also; for, though he may find himself unable to reason and meditate on the things of God, this inability may be caused by melancholy or by some other kind of indisposition having its seat in the brain or in the heart.

CHAPTER XIV

These three signs are necessary for spiritual progress
from meditation to contemplation: The faculties of
sense and of spirit. The prayer of quiet.

As to the first sign—the awareness that the spiritual person,
in order to enter upon the way of the spiritual life, should
leave the way of imagination and sensory meditation when
he has come to a point where he finds no longer any taste
in it and is unable to meditate by means of discursive reasoning—there are two things which justify this change [of the
method of prayer]: the first is that in a fashion the soul
has received all the spiritual good which it is able to find in
the things of God by way of meditation and discursive thinking. That this is the case is indicated by the very fact that
it can no longer meditate discursively as before, nor can it
find in this kind of meditation the former sweetness and
taste. The second thing [which justifies this change of
method] is the fact that the soul has by now acquired both
the substance and the habit of the spirit of meditation. For
it must be remembered that it is the end or goal of meditating and reasoning on the things of God to gain some
knowledge and love of God, and each time the soul gains
such knowledge and love through meditation, it posits an
act. Now just as many acts, of whatever kind, create eventually a habit in the soul, so in like manner many of these acts
of loving knowledge become by frequent repetition so continuous that they form a habit in the soul. Let us note, however, that in many souls God brings about this same end
without the intermediary of these acts (or at least without
many such acts), by setting them in the state of contemplation immediately.

These are the reasons, then, why the soul experiences
great weariness and distaste when, having already arrived

at this state of tranquillity, it is made to meditate and labor in particular acts of knowledge. And there are many who act in this manner when they have already begun to enter this state [of contemplation]. They think that all that is required of them is to continue their reasoning, trying to understand particular things by means of those images and sensible forms which cover the underlying spirit like a rind. And when they do not find these [forms and images] in that substantial and loving quietude in which their soul desires to rest, they think they are losing themselves on the wrong track and are wasting time. They are indeed losing themselves, but not in the way they think: they are becoming lost to their own senses and to their former manner of perception and understanding. But this kind of loss means that they are gaining a new kind of spirituality which is now being given to them. And the less they understand, the more deeply they penetrate into that night of the spirit through which they must pass in order to be united with God, in a union that surpasses all knowledge.

As to the second sign, there is little to say, for it is evident that at a time like this the soul cannot possibly take pleasure in worldly images, since, as we have stated, and for the aforementioned reasons, it takes not even pleasure in the images of God. Only, as has also been noted above, in this state of recollection the imaginative faculty is in the habit of going and coming and assuming different shapes of its own accord, that is, not according to the pleasure or at the will of the soul; on the contrary, the soul suffers pain [from these movements of the imagination], because its peace and joy are being disturbed.

Nor do I think it necessary to say much here concerning the fitness and necessity of the third sign whereby the soul may know whether the time has arrived to leave behind meditation—namely, a general loving knowledge of God and a rapt attentiveness to Him. For something has been said of this in our discussion of the first sign, and we shall have to say more about it later. Suffice it therefore to speak here of one reason only why at the time the contemplative has to leave behind the way of meditation and discursive reasoning he stands in need of this general loving attentiveness or knowledge of God. And this is the reason: if the soul at that time had not this knowledge of God or this absorption in His presence, the result would be that it would do nothing and have nothing; for, having left behind meditation (by means of which the soul has been engaged in discursive reasoning through its faculties of sense), and not being as yet in the state of contemplation (wherein the soul activates its spiritual faculties—memory, understanding, and will, in unison), the soul would of necessity be completely inactive in the things of God, since it can neither work nor receive what has been worked in it, save by way of the faculties of sense and of spirit. For, as we have pointed out, by means of the faculties of sense the soul can reason and search and gain knowledge of the objects of sense; and by means of the spiritual faculties it can have fruition of the knowledge it has already received [through the faculties of sense], although the faculties are now no longer actively in operation.

And thus the difference between the operation of these two kinds of faculties is the same as exists between laboring and enjoying the fruits of one's labor; or between the effort involved in travelling and the rest and tranquillity that are experienced upon reaching one's destination; or between preparing a meal and enjoying the taste of an already prepared meal, without having any of the labor of cooking it; or between receiving something and benefiting from that which has been received.

It is necessary, however, to emphasize that the kind of general knowledge of which we are here speaking is at times so subtle and delicate—especially when it is most pure and simple and perfect, most spiritual and most interior—that the soul is not even consciously and clearly aware of it and thus finds it most obscure. And, contrariwise, when this knowledge is least pure and simple, it appears to the understanding most clear and of major importance, because it is then clothed in certain intelligible forms which can be seized upon by the understanding or by the senses.

Now when this general and supernatural light strikes thus purely and simply, the soul is then already so completely detached and removed from all intelligible forms (which are objects of the understanding) that this light is neither felt nor seen. Rather, this light—precisely when it is purest—causes at times darkness in the understanding, because it alienates the understanding from its accustomed lights, from forms and phantasms. But when this Divine light strikes with less force, the soul neither experiences darkness nor perceives light, nor apprehends anything that it knows. And thus the soul remains at times in a state of forgetfulness, so that it knows neither where it has been nor what it has done, nor has it any awareness of the passage of time. It may and does happen, therefore, that the soul spends many hours in this forgetfulness, and when it finally returns to itself it seems as if less than a moment had passed and as if nothing at all had happened.

It seems to the soul, then, that this kind of prayer is very brief, although it may actually, as we have stated, continue for a long period of time; for the soul has been abiding in the purity of the intellect, which is above time. And this is that brief prayer of which it is said that it pierces the heavens; and when the soul awakens, this knowledge leaves in it those effects which were created in it during this state of unconsciousness—namely, the elevation of the spirit to the Divine intellect, and the alienation and withdrawal of the spirit from all things, forms, and figures, and from the remembrance of them. The soul thus remains as though it were ignorant of all things, since it knows only God, but without knowing how. Wherefore the Bride declares in the *Canticles* that among the effects which her sleep and forgetfulness produced in her was this unknowing (cf. Cant. 6:11). For although, as we have said, it seems to the soul as if in this kind of knowledge it were doing nothing at all

—because neither its senses nor its faculties are consciously occupied—it should rest assured that it is not wasting time. And this is why the Bride, who was wise, says in the *Canticles:* "I am asleep, yet my heart is awake" (Cant. 5:2). As though she were saying: although my natural self is asleep and has ceased its labors, my heart is awake, being lifted up supernaturally, in supernatural knowledge.

It should be realized, however, that it would be wrong to assume that this kind of knowledge causes of necessity this forgetfulness; for this comes about only when God suspends in the soul the exercise of all its natural and spiritual faculties, a thing which happens very rarely. And the reason why this knowledge is designated as general and loving lies in the fact that just as knowledge is communicated to the understanding obscurely, so sweetness and love are communicated to the will confusedly, so that the soul cannot have a clear and distinct knowledge of the object of its love. And thus it is evident that, as the theologians say in accord with Aristotle, the higher and more sublime the Divine light is, the darker it is to our understanding.

CHAPTER XV

Even those already advanced in the spiritual life
may at times derive benefit from natural meditation.
The nature of infused contemplation.

It should not be assumed that those who are beginning to experience this loving knowledge must, generally speaking, never try to return to meditation; for, at the time they are first beginning to make progress, the habit of contemplation is not yet so perfect that they can posit in themselves this act whenever they desire; nor have they progressed as yet so far beyond meditation that they cannot occasionally meditate and reason in the natural and accustomed way and discover something new in those diverse figures and steps of which they had made use before. Rather, until they reach a more advanced stage of the contemplative life, they do well to use sometimes the one and sometimes the other [kind of prayer].

The soul, then, will frequently find itself in this loving and peaceful attentiveness without in any way making use of its faculties and without working actively, but only by way of passive receptivity. But in order to reach this state, the soul will frequently have to make discreet and moderate use of discursive meditation. Once, however, the soul is placed in the state of contemplation, it acts no longer with its faculties; and so it would be more correct to say that the insight of the intellect and the sweetness of the will are at work within it rather than that the soul works anything at all; for its only remaining activity is its love of God, but without a desire to feel or see anything. And in this state [of contemplative love] God communicates Himself to the soul passively, in the manner in which light is communicated passively to a person who has his eyes open, without his doing more than merely to keep them open. Thus, what is meant by *passive understanding* is this reception of a light that is infused supernaturally. And when we say that the soul does not work, we do not mean that it has no understanding but that what it understands are not things which it has discovered by its own exertion; for in these illuminations, enlightenments or inspirations of God the soul receives only that which is given to it. Wherefore if at this time the will desires to understand and consider particular things, however spiritual they may be, it will thereby obstruct the pure and simple light of the spirit. Hence it is evident that when the soul has purified and emptied itself of all forms and images that can be apprehended, it will remain in that pure and simple light and will be transformed therein into a state of perfection.

When, therefore, the spiritual person is no longer able to meditate, let him learn to rest calmly in loving attention upon God, in the tranquillity of his understanding, even though it may seem to him that he is doing nothing. For thus, little by little, and indeed very soon, Divine calm and peace will be infused into his soul, together with a wondrous and sublime knowledge of God, enclothed in Divine love.

CHAPTER XVI

Imaginary supernatural visions should not be desired.

Now that we have treated of the apprehensions which the soul can receive within itself in a natural manner, and on which fancy and imagination can work by way of discursive meditation, it is fitting that we discuss next those supernatural apprehensions which are called *imaginary visions;* they likewise pertain to these [internal] senses, since they too belong to the category of images, forms, and figures.

By the term "imaginary vision" we wish to designate all things that can be represented supernaturally by means of images, forms, figures, and species. For all the apprehensions and species which are presented to the soul and dwell in it after a natural manner by means of the five bodily senses, may likewise be presented to the soul and enter it in a supernatural manner, without any assistance of the external senses. And this sense of fancy, together with memory, is like an archive or a storehouse of the understanding, in which are received all intelligible forms and images, so that the soul, having received them supernaturally by way of the five senses, bears them within itself as in a mirror. It then presents them to the understanding, which in turn considers and judges them. But even beyond this, the soul can also imagine and compound others that bear a likeness to those which it already knows.

Now even as the five external senses present the images and species of their objects to these internal senses, so both God and the devil can present the same images and species supernaturally—in even greater beauty and perfection—

without making use of the external senses. Beneath these images, therefore, God often presents to the soul many things and teaches it much wisdom. And the devil, too, when he tries to deceive the soul, presents to it images of his own making, and these often appear in the guise of good.

Of such a nature were the visions of Pilate's wife, by which he was warned not to condemn Christ. And there are many other examples which show that persons already advanced [in the spiritual life] see more frequently imaginary visions of this kind than they see external corporeal visions. The former, as we have said, do not differ from the latter, as far as the nature and appearance of the images and species are concerned; but they do differ a great deal in the degree of their perfection and with respect to the effect which they produce; for imaginary visions are more subtle and more efficacious in the soul, inasmuch as they are not only supernatural but also more internal than external supernatural visions.

These senses of imagination and fancy are the door and entrance to the soul, and it is here that, as we have stated, the understanding picks up or sets down its goods as in a harbor or market where it stores its provisions. And this is why both God and the devil go there with their jewels of supernatural forms and images, to offer them to the understanding; although this is not the only means of which God avails Himself to instruct the soul, for He dwells in the soul by His essence [*per essentiam*] and is therefore able to accomplish the same purpose either by Himself [without intermediaries] or by some other means.

I say, then, that with respect to all these imaginary apprehensions and visions as well as with respect to any other forms and species which present themselves beneath the veil of some particular kind of knowledge, image, or form—whether they be false and induced by Satan, or whether they be recognized as true, coming from God—the understanding should not be encumbered by them or feed upon them, nor should the soul desire to receive and hold them, if it wishes to remain detached, empty, pure, and simple, as is required for the state of union. For, as God is not comprised in any image or form, nor contained in any particular kind of knowledge, the soul, in order to be united with God, must not take hold of any distinct form or any particularized knowledge.

Now it is true that these imaginary visions, like the external corporeal visions of which we have spoken, may benefit the soul by communicating to it a certain kind of knowledge, or love, or sweetness. But these effects may be produced in the soul without any desire on its part to receive these visions; for, as has also been stated above, whenever they are presented to the imagination, they infuse into the soul knowledge, love, sweetness, or whatever effects God wants them to produce. And they produce these effects in the soul passively, that is, without the soul's being able to hinder it, even if it desired to do so, just as it was not in the soul's power to obtain these effects, although it was capable of disposing itself for them by its own labor.

But now there arises the following question: If it is true that God gives supernatural visions to the soul, and yet does not want the soul to desire them or be attached to them or ascribe importance to them, why then does He give them at all, since they may indeed become the occasion of the soul's falling into many errors and perils, or, at the least, they may place obstacles in the way of the soul's further progress? And this question is all the more pertinent because God can impart and communicate to the soul spiritually and substantially all that He communicates to it by means of those sensory forms and visions of which we have spoken. This question we shall try to answer in the following chapter, for this answer involves a doctrine which is of great importance and most necessary to spiritual persons as well as to those who direct them.

Spiritual persons cannot [make progress in the spiritual life] unless they close their eyes to everything that is clear and particular in knowledge and sensory perception. For [to cite one example], although St. Peter was quite certain of that vision of glory which he saw on the occasion of Christ's Transfiguration, yet, after having described it in his second canonical Epistle, he did not want it to be regarded as an important and sure testimony, but rather, directing his listeners to faith, said: "And we have the word of prophecy, which is more certain. You do well to pay heed to that word, for it is like a lamp shining in a dark room, until the day begins to dawn" (2 Pet. 1:19). By this he means to say that we have a surer testimony than this vision of Tabor—namely, the words and pronouncements of the prophets who bear testimony to Christ, and that therefore we do well to turn to these, as to a candle that gives light in a dark room. If we will ponder the meaning of this comparison, we shall find in it the doctrine which we are here espousing. For when St. Peter tells us to look to that faith of which the prophets spoke as to a candle that illumines a dark room, he is advising us to remain in darkness, keeping our eyes closed to all other lights; and he is saying that in this darkness faith alone—which is likewise dark—will be the light to which we must cling; for if we desire to cling to the sheen of these other lights—that is, to the distinct objects of intellectual knowledge—we cease to rely upon that dark light of faith, and we no longer see that light in the dark room, of which St. Peter speaks. This room, which here signifies the understanding, must remain dark until the clear vision of God dawns on it at the break of day of the life to come, or until there arrives in this life the day of transformation and union, toward which the soul is travelling.

CHAPTER XVII

God communicates to the soul spiritual goods by means of the senses because He takes into account the human mode of understanding and wants to lead the soul gradually from sense to spirit.

[In the preceding chapter] we asked the following question: Since these supernatural visions are beset with so many dangers and impediments to progress, why does God—Who is most wise and therefore eager to remove stumbling blocks and snares from the path of the soul—offer and communicate these visions to the soul?

To answer this question, we do well to set down first of all three basic principles: The first is enunciated by St. Paul, in his Epistle to the Romans, where he says: *"Quae autem sunt, a Deo ordinatae sunt"* (Rom. 13:1). This means that the works which are done are ordained by God. The second is pronounced by the Holy Spirit in the Book of Wisdom, where we read: *"Disponit omnia suaviter"* (Wisd. 8:1). This is to say that the wisdom of God, though it extends from end to end—that is, from one extreme to another —orders all things in sweetness. The third is contained in the teaching of the theologians, who say: *"Omnia movet secundum modum eorum."* That is, God moves all things according to their mode of being.

It is clear, then, in accordance with these basic principles, that if God wants to move the soul and raise it from the extreme depth of its lowliness to the extreme height of His loftiness, to Divine union with Him, He must do so with order and sweetness and in accordance with the soul's mode of being. Now the orderly and ordinary manner whereby the soul acquires knowledge is by way of the forms and images of created things, and the mode in which the soul acquires its knowledge and wisdom is by means of the senses. It follows from this that if God wants to raise

the soul to the highest kind of knowledge, and if He wants
to do so with sweet gentleness, He must begin His work
at the lowly extreme of the sensory life of the soul, so that
He may lead it, in accord with its own mode of being, to
the other extreme of His spiritual wisdom, which is above
and beyond sense. He therefore first leads the soul onward
—now naturally, now supernaturally—instructing it by
means of forms and images, and in ways of sensory perception proportionate to its own mode of understanding, and
also by means of discursive reasoning, until it finally reaches
the loftiness of the spirit of God.

This, then, is the reason why God gives the soul visions
and palpable forms, images and other kinds of sensory as
well as intelligible spiritual knowledge. This does not mean,
however, that God would not wish to give spiritual wisdom
to the soul immediately and in one single act, if the two
extremes—that is, the human and the Divine, sense and
spirit—could in the ordinary way meet and unite in one
single act, without the intermediary of many preceding preparatory acts which, as natural agents, are sweetly and har-
moniously ordered among themselves and serve as a foundation and preparation one for the other. In this manner
God leads man to perfection in accordance with the human
mode of being, starting from what is lowest and most external and guiding him to what is highest and most internal.
He therefore perfects first man's bodily senses, prompting
him to make use of good natural objects which, though perfect, are exterior, such as listening to sermons, attending
masses, looking at sacred objects of devotion, mortifying the
sense of taste at meals, and the sense of touch by penance
and holy rigor. And when these senses are thus to some
extent properly disposed, He may then perfect them still
further by bestowing upon them some supernatural favors
and gifts, so that they will become more strongly confirmed
in the good. To this end He now offers them certain supernatural communications, such as visions of saints or sacred
objects, all clothed in corporeal form, or sweetest fragrances,

locutions, and the greatest delights of touch. And by means of all this the senses are more strongly grounded in virtue and alienated from the desire for evil things. But, in addition, God continues at the same time to perfect and habituate in the good the internal bodily senses—such as imagination and fancy—by means of sacred reflections, speculations, and meditations; and in all of this He is instructing the spirit. When, however, these [internal senses] are properly disposed by this natural exercise, God may then illumine and spiritualize them still more by means of certain supernatural visions, which are those that we are here calling imaginary.

And in this manner God leads the soul step by step to the greatest degree of inwardness. This does not mean, however, that it is always necessary for God to observe this order in regard to the progress of the soul, from the first step to the last; for sometimes He places the soul in one stage and not in another, or He leads the soul from greater to less inwardness, or He may grant the soul the attainment of two stages of progress simultaneously. All this depends on what in God's judgment befits a particular soul, or on His desire to grant a soul favors of a particular kind. Nevertheless, God's ordinary way of leading a soul proceeds in the manner we have described.

Now the more strongly a thing attaches itself to one extreme, the farther it is removed and withdrawn from the other; and when it is attached completely to the one, it will be completely separated from the other. This is the meaning of the frequently quoted spiritual adage, *"Gustato spiritu, desipit omnis caro,"* that is to say, after the soul has once tasted the sweet savor of the spirit, everything carnal appears insipid. And this is obvious: for that which is spirit has no longer any share in sense; and that which can be comprehended by sense is not yet pure spirit.

The spirit, therefore, when it has attained perfection, pays no longer heed to sense, nor does it receive anything through sense, nor does it any longer have to avail itself of the ministrations of sense, as was the case prior to the attainment of this state of spiritual perfection. This is the message St. Paul means to convey when he says in his Epistle to the Corinthians: "When I was a child, I talked like a child, I had the knowledge of a child and the thoughts of a child; but when I became a man, I abandoned my childish ways" (1 Cor. 13:11). Now we have already explained how the things of sense, and the knowledge which the spirit can derive from them, are like the playthings with which a child diverts itself. If the soul then should desire to cling to them for ever, and not to cast them aside, it would never cease to be an immature child; it would go on speaking of God, knowing of God, and thinking of God in the manner of a child; for, clinging to the husk of sense (an attitude which resembles the state of childhood), it never attains to the substance of the spirit (which resembles the state of perfect manhood). And thus the soul should not desire to receive these aforementioned revelations, even though God offer them to it.

But now you may perhaps say that the soul must desire these things as long as it is immature, and that it must abandon them when it has grown up; even as a child has need of the breast to nourish itself, until it is old enough to sustain himself without the breast. To this I answer that, as far as meditation and natural discursive thinking are concerned—by means of which the soul begins its search for God—it is true that the soul should not leave the breast of sense until the proper time has arrived, that is, until God enters into that more spiritual communion with the soul which is contemplation (cf. chap. 13, *supra*). But when it is a question of imaginary visions or other supernatural apprehensions, which can enter the senses without the exercise of man's free will, I say that the soul should never desire to receive them, regardless of whether it be in the state of perfection or in a less perfect state—not even when it appears certain that they come from God. And this for two reasons: first, because, as we have said, God produces His effects in the soul without its being able to hinder it (although the soul can and may prevent visions). For, as we have also stated, the soul cannot keep out the goods which God wishes to communicate to it, except by some imperfection or attachment; and when the soul renounces these things with humility and misgivings, it thereby manifests neither imperfection nor attachment. Second, [in renouncing these things] the soul frees itself from the danger and labor involved in the attempt to distinguish between good and evil visions and to discern whether the apparition is an angel of light or of darkness.

We must then remain cognizant of the fact that the soul should never set its eyes on the husk of these figures and objects which are placed before it supernaturally, regardless of whether they are presented to the external senses—as in the case of locutions and audible words, optical visions of saints of radiant beauty, fragrant scents, tastes that are sweet to the palate, or delights that enchant the sense of touch—or whether it is a question of visions presented to the interior imaginative senses. The soul must set its eyes only upon the spiritual effect which such visions produce, and it must strive to preserve this spiritual effect in good works and to practise whatever is required for the service of God. In this way the soul takes from these things only that which God intends and desires, namely, the spirit of devotion.

CHAPTER XVIII

Certain spiritual directors may do harm to souls by using the wrong method with respect to these visions.

It will not be superfluous to expound this doctrine [concerning supernatural visions] in somewhat greater detail and to speak more distinctly about the harm that may ensue for both the spiritual souls themselves and for the spiritual directors who guide them, if either of them are too credulous with respect to these visions, even though they be of Divine origin.

The reason which has prompted me to write more at length about this matter is the lack of discretion which I have observed in certain spiritual directors. Being of the opinion that these supernatural apprehensions are good and come from God, and therefore taking for granted their authenticity, these [directors as well as the souls entrusted to their guidance] have fallen into grave error.

First of all, there are some whose error is caused by the wrong way and method they are using in dealing with souls that experience such visions. Instead of guiding these souls on the road to humility, they encourage them to fix their eyes upon these visions in one way or another, and this is the reason why these souls remain without the true spirit of faith. By inducing them to speak highly of these things, they make them feel that they themselves set considerable value upon them, and, consequently, their penitents do the same. And instead of being strengthened in faith, these souls are clinging to these apprehensions and are thus not empty, free, and sufficiently detached to fly to the heights of dark faith. From this derive many imperfections, to say the very least; for the soul is then no longer truly humble but rather thinks that all this is of some importance and conducive to some good, and that it is itself held in high esteem by God; it is therefore quite pleased and satisfied with itself. And as the soul has by now become attached to this kind of communion with God, its will acquiesces and fully consents to it. Such souls are taking a natural pleasure in their own ways of thinking and thus fall into much error. Then they see perhaps that something does not turn out quite in the way they had anticipated, and they begin to wonder and in doubt ask themselves whether this thing can be of God, since it does not come about in the manner they had imagined.

Herein, then, lies a great delusion; for revelations and locutions which have God as their author do not always turn out according to human expectations and inward imaginings. They should therefore never be blindly believed or trusted, even though we should know them to be authentic Divine revelations, answers, or pronouncements.

CHAPTER XIX

*Although visions and locutions which come from God
are true in themselves, we may misinterpret them.*

For two reasons we have said that though visions and locutions which come from God are true and always certain
in themselves, they are not always so with respect to ourselves. One reason is the defective way in which we understand them; and the other reason lies in the fact that their
causes are variable or, as it were, conditional, that is, de-
pending on the fulfillment of certain conditions or accomplishments. As regards the first reason, it is clear that they
are not always what they seem to be, nor is their outcome
always as it was conceived by our manner of understanding. This is due to the fact that, since there is in God an
immeasurable vastness and depth, He employs in His prophecies, locutions, and revelations ways, concepts, and methods
of communication and presentation that differ greatly from
the common modes and patterns of our understanding. We
find frequent examples of this in the Scriptures. The prophecies and locutions of God that were communicated to many
of the ancients [in the Old Testament] did often not come to
pass as they expected, because they had understood them
after their own manner and much too literally.

Thus, in Genesis, God said to Abraham, after He had
brought him to the land of the Canaanites: "I will give you
this land" (Gen. 15:7). And when God had told him this
many times, and Abraham was by now very old, and yet
God had not given him this land, Abraham answered and
said: "Lord, whereby or by what sign shall I know that I
am to possess it?" (Gen. 15:8). Then God revealed to him
that not he in person but rather his sons, after four hundred
years, were to possess it. And thus Abraham was finally
given to understand the meaning of this promise, which in
itself was most true; for, in giving this land to Abraham's

sons, God was giving it to Abraham, because of His love for him. And thus Abraham was deluded by the way in which he had understood the promise.

In this and in many other ways souls often misunderstand locutions and revelations that come from God, because they look to their literal and external meaning; whereas, as has already been explained, God's principal intention in these matters is to reveal and convey the spirit that is contained in these messages. And the spirit—which is difficult to understand—is much richer in meaning than the letter. He, therefore, who clings to the letter, or to a locution, or to the palpable form or figure of a vision, is bound to fall into grave error and will forthwith find himself in great uncertainty and confusion, because he has taken sense as his guide and has not allowed the spirit to work in detachment from sense. For, according to St. Paul, "The letter kills, but the spirit gives life" (2 Cor. 3:6). In this matter of sense, therefore, the letter must be rejected, and the soul must remain in the darkness of faith, which is the spirit, and it cannot be comprehended by sense.

It is clearly seen, then, that though certain pronouncements and revelations may have God as their author, we cannot always put our trust in them, since we may very easily be greatly deceived by our manner of understanding them. For they all originate in the abysmal depth of the spirit, and to try to limit them to what we can understand concerning them, and to what our senses can comprehend, is like trying to grasp the air, and to seize some particle in it that our hand touches: the air vanishes, and our hand remains empty.

The teacher of the spiritual life should therefore make his pupil turn away from all visions and locutions and impress upon him the necessity of abiding in the liberty and darkness of faith, wherein are received the liberty and abundance of the spirit, and consequently the wisdom and insight necessary for the proper understanding of the words of God. For it is impossible for a non-spiritual man to judge of the things of God or to understand them in a reasonable way; and a man is not spiritual when he judges these things according to sense. This is well expressed by St. Paul when he says: "The animal man does not perceive the things that are of the spirit of God, for they are folly to him; and he cannot understand them because they are spiritual; but the spiritual man judges all things" (1 Cor. 2:14). By the animal man is here meant one who uses sense alone; and by the spiritual man is meant one who is neither bound nor guided by sense. Wherefore it is presumptuousness to aspire to communion with God by way of a supernatural apprehension mediated by sense, or to allow others to do so.

Take, for example, a soul that greatly desires to be a martyr. It may happen that God answers, saying: You shall be a martyr. This answer will give that soul great inner joy and confidence that his desire for martyrdom will be fulfilled; yet it may come to pass that he dies not the death of a martyr, and nevertheless the promise may be true. Why, then, is the promise not fulfilled literally? Because it will be and can be fulfilled according to its principal and essential meaning in that God will give that soul the love and the reward that belong essentially to a martyr; and thus in truth He gives to this soul what it formally desired and what God promised it. For the principal desire of that soul was not a particular manner of death but rather to offer to God the service of a martyr and to show its love for Him in the manner a martyr does. For that particular manner of death is of no value without this love, and this love—its practical manifestation and the reward belonging to the martyr—God may give to the soul more perfectly by other means. And thus, although this soul may not die like a martyr, it is well satisfied that God has given it what it desired.

In this and other ways, then, the words and visions coming from God may be true and certain, and yet we may misinterpret them because of our inability to understand them in their deepest and most essential meaning, that is, in the meaning and purpose which God has intended with them.

And thus it is safest and surest to make souls flee prudently from these supernatural things and to lead them instead, as we have said, to purity of spirit in dark faith, which is the means of Divine union.

CHAPTER XX

*Though the words of God are always true, the
conditions which cause their pronouncement
may change.*

We have now to examine the second reason why visions and words which have God as their author, though always true in themselves, are not always equally certain in relation to us. This is so on account of the underlying causes, for the words of God are often based on the conditions and situations of creatures and on the effects of their actions, and these are all unstable and may be found wanting, so that for this reason the pronouncements which are founded upon them may also be subject to change and fall short of fulfillment. God may say, for example: A year hence I shall have to send upon this kingdom such or such a calamity. In this instance the cause on the basis of which this warning is pronounced is a certain offense which is being committed against God in that particular kingdom. Now if the offense ceases or is abated, the punishment too may be stayed or altered; and yet the threat was real and true because it was based on an actually committed offense, and if the offense had continued, the punishment would have been inflicted.

This is precisely what happened in the city of Nineveh, where God said: "Another forty days, and Nineveh shall be destroyed" (Jon. 3:4). This was not fulfilled, because the cause of the warning ceased: the city did penance for its sins. But if the people of Nineveh had not done penance, then the saying would have been fulfilled.

God also often declares, teaches, and promises things, not that they may be understood or possessed at that particular time, but that they may be understood at some future time when the soul will have acquired sufficient insight or when the desired effect will have been attained. This He did with His disciples, to whom He spoke in many parables and general maxims, the wisdom of which they understood not until the time when they had to embody it in their preaching, which was when the Holy Spirit came upon them. And thus God may allow a great many particular things to pass through the soul, things which neither the soul nor its director understand until the proper time arrives.

Now you will perhaps ask me: Why does God communicate these things to us, if we are not expected to understand them or to avail ourselves of them? I have already stated that everything will be understood at its appointed time according to the mandate of Him Who made the pronouncement, and he whom God wills shall understand it; and it will then be seen that it was fitting; for God does nothing without due cause and without its being true. Let us therefore acknowledge that there is no complete understanding of the full meaning of the sayings and things of God, and that this meaning cannot—without great error and utter confusion on our part—be judged by what it seems to be. And let us put our trust not in understanding, but in faith.

CHAPTER XXI

Petitions for supernatural knowledge displease God, although He may sometimes answer them. Reason and evangelical law are sufficient for the guidance of souls.

Certain spiritual persons are confident that the curiosity they display in striving to gain some specific knowledge by supernatural means is a good thing. Because God sometimes answers their persistent petitions, they think that this is a good method and pleasing to God. Yet the truth is that, although

He may answer them, the method is not good and, far from pleasing Him, it greatly displeases Him. More than that, He is often greatly offended and angered. The reason for this is that is befits no creature to go beyond the confines which God's governance has lawfully ordained for it in the order of nature. In His governance, God has laid down certain natural and rational limits for man, and it is therefore not lawful if man desires to pass beyond these; and the desire to ascertain things or to attain to them by supernatural means is to go beyond these natural limits. Thus to seek communion with God by such extraordinary ways and methods is to tempt God.

But you may say: If it be true that God is displeased, why does He sometimes answer? I reply that it is sometimes the devil who answers. And when it is really God Who answers, then I say that He does it because of the weakness of the soul that desires to travel along that road, lest it should become disconsolate and turn backward, or lest it think that God is angry with it and should feel too much saddened, or because of yet other reasons which have to do with the weakness of that soul and which are known to God.

He gives, as we have said, to each one according to his individual mode of being; for God is like a spring of water from which everyone draws as much water as the vessel he carries will hold, and sometimes He allows a soul to draw it by these extraordinary means. But from this it does not follow that it is the normal thing to draw water in this way: only God Himself may at times permit it, when, how, and to whom He wills. This will perhaps be better understood by the following comparison: Picture the father of a family who has on his table many and different kinds of food, some of which taste better than others. Now one of the children is asking him for a certain dish, not the best, but the first that meets the child's eye, and the child asks for this particular food because it would rather eat of it than of any other. And as the father sees that the child, even if it were offered the better food, will not take it, but will insist on receiving that for which it has asked, and will not be pleased with anything else, he regretfully permits the child to have the desired food, lest it should eat no food at all and be miserable. In the same way God condescends to certain souls and grants them what is not best for them, simply because they are not willing or able to walk by any other road. And thus some souls attain to tenderness or sweetness of spirit or sense; and God grants them this because they are not fitted to partake of the stronger and more solid food of the trials of the Cross of His Son, which He would prefer them to choose rather than anything else.

Much worse, however, than the desire for spiritual favors that pertain to the sphere of sense is in my estimate the desire to know things by supernatural means; for I cannot see how a soul that has such a desire can avoid committing, at the least, venial sin, however good may be its aims, and however much progress it may have made on the road to perfection; and he who encourages such a desire and gives his consent to it, sins likewise. For there is no need for any of these things, since natural reason and the evangelical law and doctrine are quite sufficient for the guidance of souls, and there is no difficulty or adversity that cannot be resolved and remedied by these means, which are pleasing to God and of great benefit to souls. And so much should we avail ourselves of reason and evangelical doctrine that, if certain things were told us supernaturally—whether in accordance with our desire or contrary to it—we should accept only that which is wholly in harmony with reason and evangelical law. And we must accept it, not because it is revelation, but because it is reason, and we must set aside all curiosity with regard to revelations. Wherefore, in all our anxieties, trials, and difficulties, there remains to us no better and surer means than prayer and the hope that God will provide for us by using such means as He Himself chooses.

In addition to the difficulties involved in making sure that one is not going astray in respect to locutions and visions which have God as their author, there are ordinarily many locutions and visions which are wrought by the devil. For in his commerce with the soul the devil more often than not wears the same guise that God uses in His dealings with it, setting before it things that very closely resemble those which God communicates to the soul. Like the wolf in sheep's clothing among the flock, he disguises himself with such success that he can hardly be recognized. And since he says many things that are true and in conformity with reason, and which come to pass exactly as he foretells them, souls are easily deceived and think that, since they are told the truth about the future course of events, this can be the work of none other than God. For such souls know not that it is a very easy thing for one who has a clear natural light to know the causes of many things, past and future. And since the devil has a very piercing light of this kind, he can very easily deduce from such and such effects such and such causes, albeit things may not always turn out as he predicts, since all causes depend ultimately on the will of God.

Let us take an example: The devil knows that the disposition of the earth and the atmosphere, and the laws governing the sun, are constituted and arranged in such a way and to such a degree that, when a certain moment in time has arrived, these elements, according to the laws of nature which govern them, will be so disposed that they will infect people with the plague. Here you have an example of a foreknowledge of the factors that will cause pestilence. And what a stupendous feat it seems to be when the devil reveals this to a soul, saying: "A year or half a year from today there will be a pestilence," and the prediction actually happens to be correct! And yet this is a prophecy of the devil. All this, however, is a mere natural knowledge, for the possession of which it suffices that the spirit be free from the passions of the soul, as Boethius states in these words: "If you desire to know truths with the lucidity of nature, cast out joy, fear, hope, and sorrow" (cf. Migne, *Patr.,* vol. 75, p. 122).

Or [to take another example] the devil may know that a man named Peter cannot, according to the natural order of things, live more than a certain number of years, and he may foretell this; and so with regard to many other things and in so many ways that it is impossible to mention them all. The only way to free oneself from all such insinuations is to flee from all supernatural revelations, visions, and locutions. And so all that has been said serves to lend support to our main contention: it all shows clearly that it displeases God when souls crave for such visions, since He allows them to cause so many and multifarious deceptions.

CHAPTER XXII

It was lawful under the Old Covenant to ask God for supernatural knowledge, because faith and revelation were still incomplete.

We see in Divine Scripture that Moses always asked God, as did King David and all the kings of Israel, and the priests and prophets of old, concerning their wars and other matters, and God answered and spoke to them. And He was not angry but rather thought that they were doing the right thing. Why, then, should it not be under the New Law of Grace as it was under the Old Law?

To this it must be replied that the main reason why under the Old Law the enquiries that were made of God were lawful, and why it was entirely fitting that prophets and priests sought visions and revelations of God, was because at that time faith had as yet no firm foundation, nor was the Evangelical Law firmly established. And so it was necessary for them to ask and for God to answer—sometimes by words, or by visions and revelations, sometimes by figures and similitudes, or by other signs that conveyed His meaning. For all that He answered and spoke and revealed had to do with the mysteries of our faith and with things related to faith or pointing forward to it. But now that our faith has its foundation in Christ, and the Evangelical Law has been made manifest, there is no longer any reason for us to enquire in that manner, nor for Him to speak or answer as He did under the Old Law. For, in giving us, as He did, His Son, Who is His Word—and He has no other—He spoke to us all, once and for all, and there is no need for Him to say anything further.

And this is the meaning of those words with which St. Paul begins his attempt to persuade the Hebrews that they should abandon the earlier manners and ways of their communication with God (according to the law of Moses), and should set their eyes on Christ alone: "In the days of old," says St. Paul, "God spoke to our fathers in many ways and by diverse means, through the prophets; but now at last, in these days, He has spoken to us once and for all in His Son" (Heb. 1:1). Herein the Apostle declares that God has become, as it were, mute, and has no more to say, since that which He spoke in ancient times to the prophets, in part, He has now spoken in plenitude in Christ, giving us that All which is His Son.

He, therefore, who would now wish to approach God with questions, or seek any vision or revelation, would not only be acting foolishly, but would be committing an offense against God by not setting his eyes wholly upon Christ. And God might answer him in this manner: If I have told you all things in My Word, which is My Son, and I have no other word, what can I answer you now, or what can I reveal to you that is greater than this? Set your eyes on Him alone, and in Him you shall find more than what you ask and desire. For you ask for locutions and revelations, and these are only the part; but if you set your eyes on Him, you shall find the Whole, because He is My complete locution and answer and all My revelation; and I have given Him to you as your brother, companion, and teacher. For since that day when I descended upon Him with My Spirit on Mount Tabor, saying: "This is My beloved Son, in Whom I am well pleased; to Him, then, listen!" (Matt. 17:5), I have laid aside all these [former] manners of teaching and answering and have entrusted all this to Him. Listen, therefore, to Him! For I have no more faith to reveal, nor any more things to make manifest. And so we must now be guided in all things by the Law of Christ, the God-Man, and by the law of His Church, and of His ministers, in a human and visible manner, and in this way we must remedy our spiritual weakness and our ignorance, for in these means we shall find abundant medicine for all of this. Nothing, therefore, is to be believed in a supernatural way, except that which is the teaching of Christ, the God-Man, and the teaching of His ministers, who are men. And this truth is emphatically affirmed by St. Paul when he says: "Even if an angel from Heaven should preach to you a gospel other than the one we preach, let him be anathema!" (Gal. 1:8).

Confessors should therefore guide their penitents in the way of faith, teaching them to turn their eyes away from all these [supernatural] phenomena and giving them to understand how much more precious in the sight of God is one work or act of the will performed in love than all the visions and communications they may receive from Heaven. Many souls, moreover, who have never had any of these experiences have made incomparably greater spiritual progress than others who have had many of them.

CHAPTER XXIII

Four kinds of purely spiritual apprehensions: visions, revelations, locutions, spiritual feelings.

We shall now begin to discuss those four apprehensions which in chapter ten we designated as purely spiritual, namely, visions, revelations, locutions, and spiritual feelings. These we call purely spiritual because they do not—as do those that are corporeal and imaginary—communicate themselves to the understanding by means of the [external or internal] bodily senses but present themselves to the understanding, clearly and distinctly, in a supernatural manner; and they do so *passively,* which means that the soul on its part does not posit any act or operation.

Speaking broadly and in general terms, all these four types of apprehensions may be called visions of the soul; for we may designate the understanding of the soul as a seeing. And inasmuch as all these apprehensions are intelligible to the understanding, they may be called "visible" in a spiritual sense. The kind of intellectual knowledge that is formed in the understanding in correspondence with these apprehensions may thus be termed an intellectual vision. Now inasmuch as all the objects of the senses are objects of the understanding to the extent that they come within the range of truth or falsehood, it follows that, just as all that is visible in a corporeal way causes corporeal vision to the eyes of the body, so all that is intelligible causes intellectual vision to the spiritual eyes of the soul (i.e., to the understanding).

Since, however, these apprehensions present themselves to the soul in the same manner as they do to the senses, it follows that, speaking properly and specifically, we shall call that which the understanding receives in the mode and manner of seeing, a *vision;* and that which the understanding receives by apprehending and comprehending new things, we shall call a *revelation;* and that which the understanding receives in analogy to the mode of hearing, we designate as *locution;* and that which the understanding receives in the manner of a perception analogous to sense perception—such as sweet spiritual fragrances and delightful spiritual tastes— we term *spiritual feelings.* From all these the soul derives spiritual knowledge or spiritual vision, without an apprehension of any form, image, or figure of the natural imagination or fancy; rather are these things communicated to the soul directly in a supernatural manner and by supernatural means.

Of these [supernatural] apprehensions, too, we should

disencumber the understanding, leading and directing it by means of them into the spiritual night of faith and onward to Divine union. For if we encumber and dull the understanding with such matters, we place obstacles in its way to solitude and the necessary detachment from all things. Though it is true that these apprehensions are nobler, more beneficial, and much more certain than those which are corporeal and imaginary—inasmuch as they are internal and purely spiritual and less accessible to the wiles of Satan— yet the understanding may not only be encumbered by them on this road but may be greatly deluded by its lack of prudent discrimination. It may be best, however, to discuss each of these types of apprehensions in particular.

CHAPTER XXIV

Two kinds of spiritual or intellectual visions: corporeal and incorporeal substances. The different effects produced by visions that are caused by God and those induced by Satan.

I say that there are two kinds of [spiritual] visions that may be wrought in the understanding [supernaturally]. The first kind is of corporeal substances, and the second kind is of incorporeal or separated substances. The corporeal [spiritual] visions have to do with all material things that are in Heaven or on earth, which the soul is able to see, even while it is still in the body, by means of a certain supernatural illumination, deriving from God, with the aid of which it is able to see all absent things in Heaven or on earth. Thus we read in the twenty-first chapter of the Apocalypse St. John's description of the glories of the celestial Jerusalem, which he saw in the Heavens.

The second kind of [spiritual] visions, which are of incorporeal substances, cannot be seen by means of this derived illumination, but only with the aid of another and higher one, which is called the Light of Glory. And these visions of incorporeal substances, such as angels and souls, are not of this life, nor can they be seen in the mortal body; for, if God were to communicate them to the soul, in their essence, the soul would at once go forth from the flesh and would depart from this mortal life. This is why God said to Moses, when the latter entreated Him to show him His essence: "No man shall see Me and be able to remain alive" (Ex. 33:20). And thus these visions pertain not to this life, save perhaps in rare instances and for brief moments, when God's dispensation allows us to pass beyond the conditions of our natural life. When this happens, He totally withdraws the spirit [of man] from this life, while His grace sustains the natural functions of the body. This is why St. Paul—referring to the time when he saw these separated [i.e., purely spiritual] substances in the Third Heaven—says: *"Sive in corpore, nescio; sive extra corpus, nescio: Deus scit"* (2 Cor. 12:2). Carried away in rapture, he says that he knows not whether when he saw these things his spirit was in his body or separated from his body, but that God knows. Herein we see clearly that St. Paul passed beyond the limits of natural life, and that this was the work of God. Likewise we read that when God showed His essence to Moses, God told him that He would set him in the cleft of the rock and would protect him by covering him with His right hand, so that he would not die when God passed in His glory. And God did pass in His glory, and He showed Himself to Moses in one fleeting moment and protected his natural life with His right hand (cf. Ex. 33:22). But such substantial visions—as those of St. Paul and of Moses, and that of our father Elias, when he covered his face while God appeared to him in a gentle whisper—occur only very rarely and to very few; for God works such things only in those who are very strong in the spirit and in the law of God.

But though these visions of spiritual substances cannot be unveiled and clearly seen in this life by the understanding, they can nevertheless be experienced in the substance of the soul, with sweetest spiritual feelings. Of these we shall, with Divine aid, speak presently when we discuss that dark and confused mystical knowledge, wherein God is united with the soul in a most lofty and Divine manner; for, in some way, this dark and loving knowledge, which is faith, serves as a means to Divine union in this life, even as in the life to come the light of glory serves as a means to attain to the clear vision of God.

Let us, then, first treat of the visions of corporeal substances which are received in the soul spiritually and which come about in the manner of bodily visions. For, just as the eyes see corporeal things by means of a natural light, so the soul—through the understanding and by means of a supernatural light—sees those same natural things, and others as well, inwardly, according to God's will. The two kinds of vision differ only in their mode and manner, since spiritual and intellectual visions are much clearer and much more subtle than corporeal visions. For, when God wishes to grant this favor to the soul, He communicates to it that supernatural light in which the soul sees easily and most clearly the things of Heaven or of earth that God wills it to see. And it is at times as though a door were widely opened before it, through which the soul sees a light that is like a flash of lightning which, in a dark night, suddenly illumines things and causes them to be seen clearly and distinctly; and at the next moment they are in darkness again, although their forms and figures remain in the fancy.

As to their effects, these visions produce in the soul quiet, illumination, and a joy like that of glory; also sweetness, purity, love, humility, and an inclination or elevation of the spirit to God.

The devil, too, can cause these visions in the soul, by means of a certain natural light, whereby, through spiritual suggestion, he clearly presents to the mind things that are present as well as things that are absent. With respect, for example, to that passage in St. Matthew, where we read that the devil "showed Him all the kingdoms of the world and their glory" (Matt. 4:8), certain doctors say that he did it by spiritual suggestion, for it was not possible for the devil to make Christ actually see with the bodily eyes all the kingdoms of the world and their glory. Yet there is a vast difference between these visions that are caused by the devil and those that are of God. For the effects produced in the soul by the former are quite unlike the effects produced by good visions: Visions caused by the devil cause aridity of spirit, an inclination to high self-esteem, and a tendency to desire and treasure such visions; and in no wise do they produce the gentleness of humility and love of God.

None of these visions, then, inasmuch as they pertain to the sphere of creatures, with whom God has no proportionate relationship or essential congruity, can serve the understanding as a proximate means to union with God. And thus it is proper that the soul's attitude in regard to them, as in regard to the other apprehensions we have described, be strictly negative, so that it may advance by the proximate means, that is, by faith. And in this way it will come to pass that the soul will go forward, aglow with yearnings of the purest love of God, without knowing whence they come nor on what ground they rest. The fact is that, as faith has become more and more deeply rooted in the soul by means of emptiness and darkness and detachment from all things, or by spiritual poverty—for all these expressions name one and the same thing—God's love has simultaneously been infused into the soul in increasing measure and has gained firmer roots. Wherefore, the more the soul desires darkness and self-annihilation with respect to all external and internal things, the more deeply it is filled with faith and, consequently, with love and hope, since these three theological virtues go hand in hand.

In order, then, to attain to that love, gladness, and joy which such visions produce in the soul, it is requisite that the soul should have fortitude, self-denial, and love, so that it may desire to remain in emptiness and darkness with respect to all things, and to ground its joy and love in that which it neither sees nor feels, nor can feel or see in this life—namely, in God, Who is incomprehensible and above all things.

CHAPTER XXV

Two kinds of revelations.

According to the order which we are here following, we have next to discuss the second kind of spiritual apprehensions, which we have above termed *revelations* and some of which pertain to the spirit of prophecy. With respect to this, it must first be known that a revelation is nothing but the uncovering of some hidden truth or the manifestation of some secret or mystery. Thus God may cause the soul to understand something, as happens when He makes clear to the understanding the truth concerning certain things, or when He discloses to the soul certain things which He is doing or intends to do.

Accordingly, we may say that there are two kinds of revelations. The first have to do with the disclosure to the understanding of truths which are properly called intellectual knowledge or intellectual communications. The second have to do with the manifestation of secrets, and this second kind is called revelation in a stricter and more proper sense. The first kind cannot be strictly called revelations because here God causes the soul to understand "naked" truths, not only with respect to temporal things but also with respect to spiritual things, unveiling them to the soul clearly and manifestly. If I have decided to discuss these under the heading of revelations, it is, first, because they resemble revelations and are closely related to them; and, second, because I do not want to multiply terminological distinctions. Accordingly, we are now prepared to divide revelations into two classes of apprehension; the one we shall call intellectual knowledge, and the other the manifestation of secrets and hidden mysteries of God. In the following chapter we shall discuss the first kind.

CHAPTER XXVI

Intuitive knowledge of two kinds of "naked" truth.

To be able to speak properly of this intuitive knowledge of "naked" truths which is imparted to the understanding, it would be necessary that God take my hand and guide my pen; for I want you to know, dear reader, that to describe what these truths are to the soul in their essence, surpasses all words.

This kind of vision is very different from that of which we have spoken in chapter twenty-four; for it is not like seeing things with the understanding but rather consists in comprehending and seeing with the understanding the things of God—things that are, that have been, and that will be; and such a seeing is akin to the spirit of prophecy.

Strictly supernatural revelations are ineffable.

Here it is to be observed that in this kind of knowledge two types must be distinguished: the one is marked by experiences of the soul concerning the Creator, and the other by experiences concerning creatures. And though both are very delectable to the soul, yet the delight caused in it by those which relate to God is comparable to nothing whatsoever, nor are there words or terms by which it can be described. For this knowledge is of God Himself, and the delight is in God Himself. In this knowledge the soul is directly linked with God, since it has in a most lofty manner an inward perception of some attribute of God—of His omnipotence, of His might, of His goodness and sweetness, and so on; and each time the soul has such an inward perception, that which is perceived adheres to the soul. And inasmuch as this is pure contemplation, the soul clearly sees that there is no way in which it can give adequate verbal expression to this experience; and yet the abundance of delight and bliss which have been felt often causes souls to make an attempt to tell about their experience. But though at times words are used in the description of such knowledge, the soul is quite aware that it has not succeeded in expressing even part of what it has felt; for it knows that there is no adequate name to describe it. And thus St. Paul, when he was granted that exalted knowledge of God, made no attempt to describe it, saying only that it was not permitted to man to speak of it.

This Divinely inspired knowledge never concerns particular matters, since these manifestations always relate to the Supreme Beginning. And this sublime knowledge can only be communicated to a soul that attains to union with God, for this knowledge is that union; and to have this knowledge is indicative of a certain intimate contact between the soul and the Deity, so that it is God Himself Who is herein perceived and tasted. And thought He is not experienced manifestly and clearly, as in the light of glory, this touch of knowledge and delight is nevertheless so lofty and sublime that it penetrates the innermost substance of the soul; and the devil cannot interfere with it or produce a counterfeit of it, since there is none; nor can he infuse any comparable sweetness or delight, because this kind of knowledge has the savor of the Divine Essence and of eternal life.

There are, then, certain kinds of knowledge and certain intimate touches wrought by God in the substance of the soul which enrich it in such a degree that not only does one of them suffice to free the soul at once from all the imperfections which it had been unable to throw off during its entire life, but they leave the soul full of virtues and Divine blessings. And these touches are so delectable to the soul that if it received only one of them it would consider itself amply rewarded for all the trials it had suffered in this life, even if they had been immeasurable. And the soul is so greatly strengthened and envigorated that it is able and willing to suffer many things for God's sake, and its greatest suffering lies in seeing that it does not suffer more.

To this exalted knowledge the soul cannot attain by any comparative measure or by any imagination of its own, because this knowledge is higher than any human measure or imagination; and so God works it in the soul without making use of the soul's own capacities. And since this knowledge is imparted to the soul suddenly and independent of its free will, it should have no part in either desiring to have it or not to have it, but should merely be humble and resigned, and God will perform His work how and when He wills.

Now as far as these apprehensions are concerned, I do not say that the soul should behave in the same negative manner as in regard to the others, since they are, as we have said, part of the union toward which we are trying to lead the soul. And this is why we are teaching the soul to empty itself of all other apprehensions. For these favors are not granted to a soul which is not completely detached. This is the meaning which the Son of God wanted to convey when He said through the mouth of St. John: "He who loves Me shall be loved by My Father, and I too will love him, and will reveal Myself to him" (John 14:21).

Prophetic visions and revelations.

The second kind of knowledge or vision of internal truths is very different from the one we have just described, since it is of things lower than God. And herein is included the knowledge of the truth of things as they are in themselves, and the knowledge of events and happenings which occur among men. This pertains to the spirit of prophecy and to that kind of grace which St. Paul calls the gift of the discernment of spirits (cf. 1 Cor. 12:10).

Concerning both kinds of intuitive knowledge we have clear testimonies in Scripture. For example, in regard to the spiritual knowledge of things the Wise Man [i.e., Solomon] says: "God has given me true knowledge of things, so that I should know the structure of the world and the powers of the elements; the beginning, middle, and end of time; the course of the sun and the change of the seasons; the cycle of the years and the constellations of the stars; the natures of animals and the furies of beasts; the powers of the spirits and the thoughts of men; the diversities in vegetation and the potency of roots; and I learned to know all things that are hidden and those that are visible, for Wisdom, the Maker of all things, taught me" (Wisd. 7:17-21). Now, although the knowledge of which the Wise Man here says that God gave it to him was infused and general, the scriptural passage furnishes sufficient evidence for all particular kinds of knowledge which God infuses into souls in a supernatural manner, whenever He wills. And though it is true that Our Lord infuses into many souls habits which relate to many things, they are of so general a kind as they were in the case of Solomon. The differences among them may be likened to those between the gifts bestowed by God which are mentioned by St. Paul, among which he distinguishes wisdom, knowledge, faith, prophecy, discernment or knowledge of spirits, the understanding of tongues, the interpretation of spoken words, and so on. All these kinds of knowledge are infused habits which God gives freely to whom He wills, sometimes naturally and sometimes supernaturally: naturally, as to Balaam, to other idolatrous prophets, and to many sybils, to whom He gave the spirit of prophecy; supernaturally, as to the holy prophets, the apostles, and other saints.

But over and above these freely bestowed habits or graces, we say that persons who are perfect or who are making progress in perfection are apt to receive enlightenment and knowledge of things present or absent; and these they get to know through the light which they receive in their spirit, which is already enlightened and purged.

And it must be known that those whose spirit is purged

can with great facility learn to know by natural means—
and some more easily than others—what is in the heart
or inward spirit [of others], and also the inclinations and
natural endowments of men, by means of outward indications, such as words, movements, and other signs. For just
as the devil can do this, since he is spirit, so can the spiritual
man, according to the words of the Apostle: "The spiritual
man can judge all things" (1 Cor. 2:15). And again St.
Paul says: "The spirit penetrates to the depth of things,
even to the deep things of God" (1 Cor. 2:10). Wherefore,
although spiritual persons cannot by nature know thoughts
or what is hidden in the minds of others, they may be able
to gain such insight through supernatural illumination or by
means of signs. And yet we must trust neither to the one
means nor to the other, for the devil meddles herein greatly
and with much subtlety, and we should therefore always
renounce these kinds of knowledge.

Now all such knowledge comes about in the soul passively, without any activity on its part; for it will happen
that while a person is inattentive or absent-minded, there
will come to him a vivid understanding of what he is reading or hearing, an understanding much clearer than could
ever be conveyed by the sound of words; and at times,
though he does not understand the words—as when they
are in Latin and he does not know Latin—the knowledge
of their meaning is conveyed to him.

With regard to the deceptions which the devil can and
does bring about concerning this kind of knowledge and
understanding, a great deal might be said, since the de-
lusions which he works in this way are great and hard to
recognize as such. Inasmuch as, through suggestion, he can
present to the soul many kinds of intellectual knowledge
and implant them so firmly that they assume the appearance
of truth, he will—unless the soul be humble and wary—make
it believe a great many falsehoods. For suggestion exerts
great power upon the soul. [When this happens], the soul

must have recourse to earnest prayer, and it needs great strength to cast off [such insinuations and suggestions].

And thus all such knowledge, whether it derive from God or not, can be of very small service to the soul on its journey to God, if it clings to it with its desire. Rather, if it were not scrupulous in rejecting this kind of knowledge, it would not only be hindered in its progress, but it would even be greatly harmed and led into grievous error.

CHAPTER XXVII

The second type of revelations: the unveiling of hidden secrets.

We were saying that the second type of revelations was the manifestation of hidden secrets and mysteries. This can come about in two ways: first, concerning that which God is in Himself, and therein is included the revelation of the mystery of the Most Holy Trinity and Unity of God; and, second, concerning that which God is in His works, which includes the other articles of our Catholic faith as well as those propositions which—on the basis of the articles of faith—can be explicit established as truths. Comprised therein are a great number of the revelations given to the Prophets, certain promises or ominous warnings of God, and other things which have happened or are to happen. To this second category belong also many other particular things which God reveals at certain times, both concerning the universe in general as also in particular concerning certain kingdoms, provinces, estates, families, and individuals. Of all this we have an abundance of examples in the Scriptures, especially in all the Prophets. And these revelations are not confined to words alone, but God gives them in many ways and manners, sometimes indeed by words alone, sometimes, however, solely by means of signs and figures, or by images and similitudes, and at other times in several ways simultaneously, as is particularly seen throughout the Apocalypse, where we find all the types of revelations of which we have spoken.

As to these revelations of the second type, God grants them even in our time to whom He wills. Sometimes, for example, He reveals to some persons how many days they still have to live, or what trials they have to undergo, or what fate is in store for such and such a person, or such and such a kingdom, and so on. And even with respect to the mysteries of our faith He may unveil and explain their truths to the spirit, although this cannot properly be termed "revelation"—inasmuch as these mysteries have already been revealed—but is better called a manifestation or exposition of truths already revealed.

In this kind of revelations the devil may take a strong hand. For, as revelations of this nature are ordinarily clothed in words, figures, or similitudes, the devil can easily simulate them, much more so than when the revelations are purely spiritual. And therefore, if in matters of faith anything new or different be "revealed" to us, we must in no wise give our consent to it, even though we had evidence that the words spoken were those of an angel from Heaven.

Since, then, there are no more articles to be revealed concerning the substance of our faith than those which have already been revealed to the Church, the soul must close its understanding [to such "revelations"] and must simply adhere to the doctrine of the Church and to its faith. For even if it were true that there was no peril in such deception, it does not behoove the soul to desire a clear understanding of the things of faith, so that it may preserve the merit of faith in its purity and entirety and may in this night of the understanding attain to the heavenly light of Divine union.

CHAPTER XXVIII

Internal [supernatural] locutions.

The third kind of apprehensions [of which we are here speaking] is *supernatural locutions*. They are apt to be wrought in the spirit of spiritual persons without the intermediary of any bodily sense. Although they are of many kinds, they may, I believe, all be reduced to three particular types which I call successive, formal, and substantial. *Successive* I term certain words and rational arguments which the spirit forms and considers when it is inwardly recollected. *Formal words* are certain clear and formally distinct words which the spirit receives, not of itself, but from a third person, sometimes when it is recollected and sometimes when it is not. *Substantial words* are words which are likewise formed in the spirit, either when it is or when it is not in a state of inward recollection. And these [three types] we shall now discuss in due order.

CHAPTER XXIX

Successive words which the recollected spirit sometimes forms within itself may proceed from one of three causes: (1) from the Divine spirit; (2) from the natural light of the understanding; (3) from Satan.

Successive words always are formed when the spirit is recollected and very attentively absorbed in some meditation. By its reasoning it then discovers certain things which are related to its reflections and which it did not know previously, so that the spirit is led to believe that this is not its own work, but that it is another person who does its reasoning, answers its questions, or teaches it. And in truth it has good cause to think that this is so, for the spirit is here arguing with itself and answering itself as though one person were speaking with another; and in some way this is actually the case; for, although it is the spirit itself which works as an instrument, the Holy Spirit often comes to its aid in the production and formation of those true concepts, words, and arguments. And since at that time the understanding is recollected and united with the truth of that whereof it is thinking, and since the Divine Spirit is likewise united with it in that same truth (as it is always united with every truth), it follows that the understanding begins to form within itself successively those other truths which are related to that whereof it was thinking. And it is the Holy Spirit Who, thus opening the door to the understanding, continually enlightens and instructs it. And when the understanding is thus illumined and taught by this Master, and comprehends these truths, it begins to form of its own accord the words which relate to the truths that are communicated to it from elsewhere, so that we may say that the voice is the voice of Jacob, but the hands are the hands of Esau.

Now though it is true that in this kind of communication and in this illumination of the understanding no deception is produced in the soul itself, yet deception may and often does enter into the formal words and rational arguments which the understanding bases on such communications. For since at the outset the soul began to take hold of the truth, and then brought to bear on it the ability or the ineptitude of its own lowly understanding, it is easy to see why the interpretation that is given varies in accordance with the intellectual capacity of the individual soul.

I am appalled at what so often happens in our day: When some soul with very limited experience in meditation becomes conscious of certain locutions of this kind, it forthwith christens them all as coming from God, saying: "God told me," or "God answered me"; and in reality it is not so at all, but, as we have said, in the majority of cases these souls have merely been talking to themselves.

The desire, moreover, which people have for locutions, and the way in which their spirits become attached to them, cause them to make answer to themselves and then to think that it is God Who is answering them and speaking to them. What results from this is mere prattle and impurity of soul rather than humility and mortification of spirit. They think that what they have experienced was a great thing, whereas in reality it was little more than nothing, or nothing at all, or less than nothing. For what can be the value of something that does not engender humility, love, mortification, silence, and holy simplicity?

The understanding cannot find any greater recollection than in faith; and it is in faith, therefore, that the Holy Spirit will give it the greatest illumination. For the purer and more refined in faith the soul has become, the more it has received of the infused love of God; and the more love it has, the more it is illumined and filled with the gifts of the Holy Spirit, since love is the cause and the means by which these gifts are communicated to it.

In this type of locution, that is, in successive internal words, the devil frequently plays an active part, especially in the case of persons who have some inclination or affection for these locutions. For at the time when they begin to be recollected, the devil often offers them ample material for distractions, forming concepts or words in their understanding by way of suggestion, and then confounding and deceiving it most subtly with things that have the appearance of truth.

Criteria to judge the origin of locutions.

From what has been said it is evident that these successive locutions may proceed in the understanding from three causes: (1) from the Divine Spirit, Who moves and illumines the understanding; (2) from the natural light of the understanding; and (3) from the devil, who may speak to the soul by suggestion. To describe the signs and indications by which it may be known whether they proceed from one cause or another would be somewhat difficult, but it is quite possible to name some general signs: When the soul finds that it is loving God in its words and thoughts and if simultaneously its love is joined with the spirit of humility and reverence, it is a sign that the soul is moved by the Holy Spirit. When, on the other hand, the locutions proceed solely from the vigor and light of the understanding, then everything is the work of the understanding. And when the meditation is over, the will remains dry, though not inclined to either vanity or evil, unless the devil should assail it with new temptations. This, however, is not the case when the locutions were caused by a good spirit; for then, as a rule, the will remains afterwards lovingly affixed to God and inclined toward the good. But occasionally it will happen nevertheless that the will remains dry, although the communication has been wrought by a good spirit, since God ordains it so for reasons that benefit the soul. We see, then, that it is sometimes difficult to recognize the difference between the several kinds of locutions, owing to the varied effects which they produce; but those we have now described are the most common.

Let us remember, then, that great caution is necessary, so that we may not be deceived or encumbered by these locutions. And let us not hold any of them in high esteem, but learn to direct our will to God with firm determination, fulfilling His law and His holy counsels perfectly, for this is the wisdom of the saints.

CHAPTER XXX

Internal words that are supernaturally infused into the spirit.

The second type of internal words are *formal words,* which are occasionally produced in the spirit by supernatural means, without the intermediary of any of the senses—sometimes when the spirit is recollected and at other times when it is not. I call them "formal" because they are formally addressed to the spirit by a third person, while the spirit itself plays no active part in this. They differ therefore greatly from the locutions we have just described.

Now these words are sometimes more and sometimes less clearly formulated; for they are frequently like concepts by means of which something is verbally communicated to the spirit, sometimes in the nature of a reply and sometimes in another mode of speaking. Sometimes only one word is heard, sometimes there are two or more, and at other times the words succeed one another as was the case with those we have already described.

When these words are no more than formal, the effect which they produce in the soul is not very great. But when they come from God they produce in the soul a quick and lucid readiness to do whatever it is commanded or instructed to do. And yet at times they do not take from the soul the repugnance and the difficulties which it feels but rather tend to increase them. When this happens, it is because God wants to further the good of the soul by instructing it better and by teaching it greater humility. And such repugnance is felt most commonly when God commands the soul to do things of a high order, or things which may demand the activation of the soul's highest qualities. When, on the other hand, it is a question of the fulfillment of low and humble tasks, the soul responds with greater ease and speed.

To all these formal words the soul must attach no more importance than to successive words; for, aside from the fact that to do so would preoccupy the spirit with matters which are not legitimate and proximate means to union with God, it might also very easily cause it to be deceived by the devil. For sometimes it is hardly possible to know what words are spoken by a good spirit, and what by an evil spirit. The soul, therefore, must not concern itself with exploring the meaning of these words, nor attach any importance to them, regardless of whether they come from a good or from an evil spirit. The words should rather be reported to an experienced confessor or to some other discreet and learned person, who may then give proper instruction and counsel, and decide what is to be done in this matter.

CHAPTER XXXI

Substantial words that are internally communicated to the spirit.

The third kind of internal words we called *substantial*. Although they too are "formal," since they are impressed upon the soul with formal clarity, they differ nevertheless in that substantial words produce in the soul vivid and substantial effects, which is not so in the case of merely formal words. Though it is true, then, that every substantial word is formal, not every formal word is substantial. Only then is a word substantial when it substantially impresses upon the soul that which it signifies. If, for example, Our Lord were to say to the soul in a formal manner: "Love Me," the soul would presently have and feel within itself the substance of love for God. Or if the soul were in great fear, and God said to it: "Fear not," it would immediately feel great strength and tranquillity. For, as the Wise Man says, the speech and word of God is full of power (cf. Eccles. 8:4); and thus He works in the soul substantially whatever He says. So it happened with Abraham, when God said to him: "Walk in My presence and be perfect"; and he was perfect forthwith and henceforth walked in reverence before God. And this is the power of His word in the Gospel, the power with which He healed the sick and raised the dead, merely by speaking a word. And in the same manner He grants to certain souls substantial locutions of such moment and price that they are for these souls life and virtue and an incomparable good; for one of these words works more good in the soul than all that the soul has itself accomplished in its entire life.

Now with respect to these words the soul should do nothing; it should neither desire them nor abstain from desiring them; it should neither reject them nor fear them. And it should do nothing in the way of trying to practise what these words imply; for these substantial words are never spoken by God in order that the soul should of itself act upon them but rather that He Himself may work within the soul; and in this they differ from formal and successive words. Let the soul therefore practise resignation and humility with respect to substantial words. And as the soul receives these blessings passively, its action is in no way important. Nor should the soul fear any deception, for neither the understanding nor the devil can here interfere.

These substantial words perform thus a great service in leading the soul to union with God; and the more internal and substantial they are, the greater is the benefit which the soul derives from them. Happy, therefore, is the soul to whom God speaks. "Speak, oh Lord, your servant listens" (1 Sam. 3:10).

CHAPTER XXXII

Supernaturally induced spiritual feelings.

The time has now come to treat of the fourth and last kind of intellectual apprehensions which, as we have said, may enter the understanding by way of *spiritual feelings,* which are often produced supernaturally in the souls of spiritual persons.

These distinct spiritual feelings may be of two kinds. Those of the first kind reside in the affection of the will, while those of the second kind reside in the substance of the soul. Each of these may in turn be of many different types. Those residing in the will, when they are of God, are very sublime; but those which are of the substance of the soul are also very lofty and bring with them many benefits and blessings. As to these latter, neither the soul nor its director can either know or understand the cause from which they proceed, or the nature of the acts on account of which God grants these favors. For they do not depend on any good works performed by the soul, nor upon its meditations, although both of these things tend to dispose the soul for them. But God grants these favors to whom He wills and for whatever reason He wills. For it may happen that a person will have performed many good works, and yet he will not be granted these touches of Divine favor; and another will have done far fewer good works, and he will receive the most sublime favors and in great abundance. And thus it is not even necessary that the soul be actually employed and occupied in spiritual things (although it is much better for the soul to be so employed if it is to receive these favors) for God to grant it these touches.

These spiritual feelings—to the extent that they are feelings only—pertain not to the understanding but to the will; and thus I do not propose to discuss them here at length. I shall treat of them in Book Three, in the course of the discussion of the night and purgation of the will. But since in the majority of cases apprehensions and intellectual knowledge overflow from these feelings into the understanding, they should at least be mentioned here. This [apprehension of an intellectual knowledge deriving from this overflow into the understanding] is often a most sublime perception of God, and no name can be given either to this experience itself or to the feelings from which this overflow derives.

Just as the spiritual feelings which we have described are wrought in the soul passively and thus without any effective activity on the part of the soul in bringing about their infusion, so also is the knowledge of them received in the understanding passively, that is, in such a way that the understanding plays no part in the acquisition of this knowledge. The understanding, therefore, in order not to go astray and impede the benefits which come from these feelings, must do nothing with respect to them, but must remain passive and make no use of its natural capacity. For human nature is unable to attain to this most delicate knowledge by its own efforts, but only by keeping itself open and receptive to its influx. Let the soul therefore be resigned, humble, and passive, for, since it receives this knowledge from God passively, He will communicate it whenever it pleases Him, provided He finds the soul humble and detached. And in this way the soul on its part will not impede the great blessings which accrue from this knowledge and which will aid it on the way to Divine union.

BOOK THREE

*The First Dark Night of the Spirit:
Hope and Love*

CHAPTER I

*The purgation of memory and will in the first
active night.*

The first faculty of the soul—the understanding—has now been instructed in the first theological virtue, which is faith, in order that, as far as this faculty is concerned, the soul may be united with God by means of the purity of faith. It now remains to do the same with respect to the other two faculties of the soul, which are memory and will, and to purify them likewise, so that the soul may attain to union with God in perfect hope and love. This will be done with all possible brevity in this third book. It is not necessary for us to write at great length about these two faculties because it is not possible that, if the spiritual man has instructed his understanding in faith according to the doctrine which we have given him, he should not, while he is proceeding on this road, instruct these other two faculties in the other theological virtues likewise; for their operations are interdependent.

But, in order to follow our method of exposition, we shall have to set down here the apprehensions pertaining to each faculty, and first, those of the memory; and we shall make such distinctions between its apprehensions as will suffice for our purpose. These distinctions we shall be able to deduce from the distinctions among their objects, which are threefold: natural, imaginary, and spiritual. And, accordingly, there are three kinds of knowledge deriving from the memory: natural, imaginary, and spiritual. These we shall discuss in the following chapters, beginning with natural knowledge, which relates to the most external objects. Subsequently we shall deal with the affections of the will.

CHAPTER II

To be supernaturalized, the memory must be emptied of all natural apprehensions.

If it be true, as it is, that the soul on its way to God must learn to know Him by what He is not rather than by what He is, it must proceed by totally denying and refusing to accept in its apprehensions everything that can be renounced, whether this be natural or supernatural. And in this manner we shall proceed now with regard to the memory, drawing it out of its natural setting and its limitations, and raising it above itself, that is, above all distinct knowledge and apprehensible possession, and leading it to the heights of the supreme hope of the incomprehensible God.

Beginning, then, with natural knowledge, I say that natural knowledge in the memory consists of all kinds of knowledge which the memory can acquire concerning the objects of the five bodily senses. Of all these forms of knowledge the soul must strip and empty itself, and it must strive to lose the imaginary apprehension of them, so that there remains in it no impression of knowledge and no trace of anything whatsoever; rather, the soul must be naked and void, in total oblivion and suspension, as if no apprehension or form had ever passed through it. This, however, cannot happen unless the soul be totally separated from all forms which are not God. And since, as Christ says, no man can serve two masters (Matt. 6:24), and since the memory cannot be united both to God and to specific forms of knowledge, and God has no form or image that can be comprehended by the memory, it follows that, when the memory is united with God, it remains without form and without figure; its imagination is lost and it is absorbed in a supreme good and in a great oblivion in which it remembers nothing. For this Divine union voids its fancy and raises it to the supernatural.

Sometimes this oblivion of the memory and suspension of the imagination reach such a point that a long time passes without the soul's being aware of it, or knowing what has taken place. And since the imaginative faculty is then in suspension, this person loses all sensitivity and does not even feel things that normally cause pain; for without the imaginative sense there is no sensation. But it is to be noted that these suspensions do not occur in those who have reached the state of perfection, since they have attained to perfect union.

Now someone may say that, though this seems all very well, the inevitable consequence is the destruction of the natural functional use of the faculties and the reduction of man to the status of a brute, to a state of complete for-lornness and even worse, since he is no longer capable of reasoning or of remembering his natural functions and ne-cessities. It will be argued that God does not destroy nature but rather leads it to perfection, and that a destruction of nature follows of necessity when one forgets to practise what is demanded by morality and reason.

To this I reply that, as a matter of fact, the more the memory attains to union with God, the more are the spe-cific kinds of knowledge perfected within it, until the time arrives when it loses them altogether and when in perfec-tion it attains to the state of union. And thus, at the be-ginning, the soul of necessity falls into great oblivion with respect to all things, since all forms of knowledge are being eradicated from it; and it therefore becomes guilty of many neglects in its external behavior—such as forgetting to eat or drink, or being uncertain whether or not it has done, seen, or said certain things, because its memory is com-pletely absorbed in God. But when once the soul attains to the habit of Divine union, it no longer has these periods of forgetfulness in matters that pertain to natural and moral reason. On the contrary, it then performs all useful and necessary activities with a much higher degree of perfection, although it performs them no longer with the aid of forms of knowledge that pertain to the memory. For when the soul has this habit of union, which is a supernatural state, memory and the other faculties fail it completely, as far as their natural functions are concerned, because they pass beyond their natural limitations.

In this state, therefore, the operations of the memory and of the other faculties are all Divine. For, once God has taken possession of the faculties and has become their undisputed master, it is He Himself Who moves and commands them divinely, according to His Divine Spirit and will. All that the soul does is then of God, and all its actions are Divine; for, as St. Paul says, he who unites himself to God becomes one spirit with Him (cf. 1 Cor. 6:17). It is thus God alone Who moves the faculties of these souls to do those works which are desirable according to His will and command, and they cannot be impelled to do others. And thus the works and prayers of these souls are always efficacious, as were those of Our Lady, the most glorious Virgin Mary. Being raised to this high estate from the beginning, she never bore upon her soul the form and impress of any creature, but was always moved and guided by the Holy Spirit.

And the Holy Spirit enlightens such souls not only in these things, but in many others relating to both the present and the future and, in many instances, also to things and events that are far distant. Although at times this comes about by means of intellectual forms, it frequently happens without the intermediary of any apprehensible form, so that these persons know not whence their knowledge comes.

The truth is, as I said before, that God must place the soul in this supernatural state, but the soul on its part must never desist from preparing itself; and it can prepare itself by natural means, especially with the help that God is continually giving it. And thus, as the soul on its part progressively enters into this renunciation and empties itself of forms, God on His part grants it the possession of union. And this God works in the soul passively, as we shall further explain when we treat of the passive night of the soul.

CHAPTER III

The first kind of harm that may befall the soul which fails to enter into this darkness of the memory.

A spiritual person is subject to *three kinds of harm* when, in order to journey to God, he persistently desires to make use of the natural knowledge and the rational operations of the memory. Two of these are positive, and the third is privative. The first derives from the things of the world, the second comes from the devil, and the third consists in the impediments that are caused in the soul and hinder its progress to Divine union.

The *first* harm, caused by the things of the world, consists in the subjection of the soul—through knowledge and discursive reasoning—to many evils, such as falsehoods, imperfections, desires, opinions, loss of time, and many other things causing all kinds of impurities in the soul. But the soul frees itself from all of these if the memory enters into darkness with respect to all reasoning and knowledge.

You will perhaps say that by following this precept the soul deprives itself of many good thoughts and reflections concerning God, which are of great benefit and conducive to the reception of Divine favors. I answer that to this end purity of soul is the greatest of all benefits, and this consists in detachment from all creatures and from all affections for temporal goods. It is better, therefore, to learn how to silence and put to rest the faculties, so that God may speak.

In this state, then, we shut the door to all things from which distraction may come and which are a hindrance to Divine union; we cause the memory to be quiet and mute, and we allow the ear of the spirit to listen to God in silence.

Let the soul, then, remain enclosed with itself, without care and anxiety, for He Who entered in bodily form through closed doors to meet His disciples, and gave them peace (cf. John 20:19), will enter spiritually into the soul, when the doors of its faculties—memory, understanding, and will—are closed to all apprehensions.

CHAPTER IV

The harm caused by the devil.

The *second* positive harm that can be done to the soul— through the knowledge that lodges in the memory—is caused by the devil, who by this means exerts great influence upon the soul. For he can adduce ever new forms of knowledge and rational arguments and can thus induce into the soul pride, avarice, wrath, envy, unjust hatred, vain love, and manifold deception. He also frequently implants in the fancy fixed ideas, in such a manner that what is false appears to be true, and what is true, false. And it is a fact that the greatest deceptions and evils which the devil brings to the soul enter by way of the knowledge and the rational operations of the memory. If, then, the memory enters into darkness with respect to all of these things and annihilates itself in oblivion, it shuts the door firmly to this evil influence. For the devil has no power over the soul, except through the operations of its faculties and especially through the medium of knowledge. If, then, the memory annihilates itself with respect to the faculties, the devil is powerless.

CHAPTER V

The third kind of harm is privative.

The third kind of harm that may be done to the soul by the natural apprehensions of the memory is privative; for these apprehensions can impede moral good and deprive us of spiritual good. Now moral good consists in the restraining of the passions and the curbing of disorderly desires, and this induces into the soul tranquillity, peace, quietude, and moral virtues. This restraining and curbing of the passions cannot be truly accomplished by the soul unless it forgets and withdraws from the things with which it is preoccupied and which give rise to its affections; and no disturbances ever arise in the soul except through the apprehensions of the memory. For, when all things are forgotten, there is nothing that can disturb the soul's peace or move its desires, since, as the saying goes, that which the eye sees not the heart desires not.

All this we know from constant personal experience; for we observe that whenever the soul is engaged in thinking of something, it is more or less agitated and disturbed; now it is joyful, now sad; now it hates, now it loves; and it cannot continue for long in one and the same mood unless it tries to forget all things.

Again, what has been said clearly proves that an encumbered memory also impedes spiritual good; for the soul that is disturbed and has no foundation of moral good is to that extent incapable of attaining to spiritual good, which impresses itself only on souls that are tranquil and at peace. And moreover, if the soul is attached to the apprehensions of the memory, it is not possible for it to be free to adhere to the incomprehensible, which is God. For, in order to proceed on its way to God, the soul must walk by not comprehending rather than by comprehending; it must exchange the mutable and comprehensible for the immutable and incomprehensible.

CHAPTER VI

The benefits which result from forgetfulness and from the emptiness of the memory are peace of mind and freedom from temptations.

From the consideration of the different kinds of harm which come to the soul through the apprehensions of the memory, we can infer the converse benefits that result when the soul forgets these apprehensions and empties itself of them. In the first place, the soul enjoys tranquillity and peace of mind, since it is free from those disturbances and vacillations which arise from the thoughts and concepts of the memory, and consequently it enjoys purity of conscience and soul. Secondly, it is freed from many suggestions, temptations, and insinuations of the devil. Thirdly, the soul—owing to this recollection and the withdrawal from all things—is properly disposed to be moved and taught by the Holy Spirit. And even if a person received no other benefit from this forgetfulness and emptiness of the memory than being freed from anxieties and other disturbances, it would be a great gain and blessing. For it is obvious that it is always futile to disquiet oneself, since it profits no one. And thus, even if everything came to an end and were utterly destroyed, and if all things went wrong and turned out adversely, it would be futile to be disturbed, since this always does more harm than good. But to bear everything with tranquil and peaceful equanimity not only brings the soul the benefit of many blessings, but aids it, even in the midst of adversities, in judging them more realistically and in finding a fitting remedy. This is why Solomon, who was familiar with both the harm and the benefit of which we are speaking, said: I knew that it is best for man to rejoice

and do good in his life (cf. Eccles. 3:12). By this he meant
that in everything that may happen to us, no matter how
adverse it may be, we should rejoice rather than be
troubled, so that we may not lose a good that is greater
than any kind of prosperity—namely, tranquillity and peace
of mind.

CHAPTER VII

*The more the memory dispossesses itself, the more it
attains to the perfect possession of God.*

Although in writing of natural apprehensions of the first
kind we have also given instruction concerning imaginary
[natural] apprehensions, it was fitting to make this division
because of the love which the memory retains for other
forms and kinds of knowledge, which concern supernatural
things, such as visions, revelations, locutions, and feelings.
When these things have passed through the soul, there often
remains impressed upon it some image, form, figure, or
knowledge, at times very vividly and effectively.

Now we must ever bear in mind that the more attention the soul pays to any clear and distinct apprehensions,
whether they be natural or supernatural, the less capacity
and preparation it has for entering into the abyss of faith.
The soul must therefore void itself also of all these forms
and kinds of knowledge, so that it may unite itself with God
in hope. For every kind of possession is contrary to hope,
which, as St. Paul says, convinces us of things which are
not possessed (cf. Heb. 11:1). Wherefore, the more the
memory dispossesses itself, the greater is its hope; and the
greater its hope, the more it is united with God; for, with
respect to God, the more the soul hopes, the more it attains. And it hopes most when it is most completely dispossessed; and when it is totally dispossessed, it remains
with the perfect possession of God, in Divine union. For

he who renounces not all that he possesses cannot be a
disciple of Christ (cf. Luke 14:33).

CHAPTER VIII

*Five kinds of harm that may be caused in the soul
by the knowledge of supernatural things. The first
kind: self-deception.*

The spiritual person who pays attention to and reflects upon
these forms and kinds of knowledge which are impressed
upon him by the things that pass through his memory in
a supernatural way, exposes himself to five kinds of harm.
The *first* consists in his being frequently deceived by mis-
taking one thing for another. The *second* involves the danger
of his succumbing to some form of presumption or vanity.
The *third* consists in his giving the devil a free hand in
working deceptions by means of these apprehensions. The
fourth lies in the fact that he is hindered in his being united
with God in hope. And the *fifth* is that, for the most part,
he has a low esteem of God.

As to the *first kind of harm,* it is clear that, if a
spiritual person pays attention to these forms and kinds of
knowledge and reflects upon them, he is bound to be frequently deceived in his judgment of them; for, as no man
can have a complete understanding or judgment of the
things which pass through his mind naturally, he will have
this even less with respect to supernatural things.

In order not to succumb to this evil of being deceived
in his judgment, the spiritual person should therefore not
desire to use his judgment in trying to understand the nature of his own experiences and feelings, or the nature of
such and such a vision, such and such a kind of knowledge,
or such and such feelings. For, whatever may be their intrinsic nature, they cannot help him as much to love God

as can the smallest act of living faith and hope, performed in emptiness and in renunciation of all things.

CHAPTER IX

The second kind of harm: self-esteem and presumption.

The supernatural apprehensions of the memory already described are also a frequent occasion to spiritual persons of falling into some kind of presumption or vanity, if they pay attention to them or value them highly. From this may result a certain secret satisfaction, self-esteem, and great spiritual pride. These persons are then prone to behave like the Pharisee who gave thanks to God that he was not as other men, and that he possessed such and such virtues. And some such persons become so proud that they are worse than the devil.

In order to flee from this pestiferous evil, which is so loathsome in the eyes of God, spiritual persons must consider two things: first, that virtue consists not in apprehensions and feelings one may have concerning God, no matter how sublime they are, but, on the contrary, in that which has nothing to do with feeling—namely, great humility and contempt of oneself and of everything pertaining to oneself; and also in rejoicing that others feel the same way about us and in not wishing to enjoy any esteem in the minds of others. Second, it should be remembered that all visions, revelations, and heavenly feelings are not worth nearly as much as the least act of humility. For an act of humility has the effect of love, and the humble soul thinks not evil, except of itself; nor does it think any good thing of itself, but only of others.

CHAPTER X

The third kind of harm comes from the devil.

From all that has been said above it can be clearly understood and deduced how much harm may come to the soul from the devil by way of these supernatural apprehensions. For not only can he present to the memory and fancy many false forms and false kinds of knowledge in the guise of goodness and truth—impressing them very effectively on spirit and sense and certifying their apparent truth by means of suggestion, but he may also tempt the soul in many ways with respect to true knowledge, which comes from God, by stirring its spiritual or sensual desires and affections; for, if the soul takes pleasure in such apprehensions, it is very easy for the devil to cause its desires and affections to grow within it and to make it fall into spiritual gluttony and other evils.

The soul, blinded by that pleasure, and setting its eyes more on pleasing sensations than on love, will then give more heed to these apprehensions than to the nakedness and emptiness which are found in faith, in hope, and in the love of God. For to a soul that is blind, falsehood no longer appears to be falsehood, nor does evil appear to be evil, and so on; for darkness appears to be light, and light, darkness. And all this happens to the soul because it did not deny itself the pleasure of these supernatural things at the outset.

CHAPTER XI

The fourth kind of harm: Divine union is impeded.

Not much needs to be said concerning this fourth kind of harm, inasmuch as it has already been sufficiently described in this third book, wherein we have shown how, in order that the soul may attain to union with God in hope, it must renounce every possession of the memory; for, if all its hope is to be centered in God, it must have nothing in the memory that is not God. And no form, figure, or image, or any other kind of knowledge that can be present in the memory can be God or can be like God, whether it be natural or supernatural. And thus, if the memory desires to give heed to any of these things, it impedes the soul's progress toward God.

CHAPTER XII

The fifth kind of harm: a low esteem of God.

The soul is harmed in no less degree by the fifth evil. This is caused by the soul's desire to retain in the memory and imagination the forms and images of things which are supernaturally communicated to it. The very fact that the soul esteems these apprehensions causes it not to esteem God as highly as is required by faith, since faith teaches us that He is incomparable and incomprehensible. For creatures, whether they be of Heaven or of earth, and all distinct images and kinds of knowledge, both natural and supernatural, that can be apprehended by the faculties of the soul have no comparison or proportion with the being of God, since God is above any genus and species. And the soul in this life is not capable of receiving in a clear and distinct manner anything that does not fall within genus and species. He, therefore, who encumbers his memory and the other faculties of the soul with things which they are unable to comprehend, cannot esteem God as highly as he should.

CHAPTER XIII

The benefits which the soul derives from casting aside the apprehensions of the imagination.

The benefits which derive from emptying the imagination of all imaginary forms can be gauged by the five kinds of harm which these forms cause in the soul, if it desires to retain them. But there are yet other benefits for the spirit, such as great peace and quietude.

But perhaps you will say: Why do many spiritual persons advise the soul to try to profit by communications and feelings that come from God? And why does St. Paul say: "Do not stifle the spirit?" (Thess. 5:19). And why does the Spouse say to the Bride: "Hold me close to your heart and set me as a seal upon your arm?" (Cant. 8:6). For it seems to be obvious that, since God is the giver of these things, He must give them for a good purpose, and the effect must be good. And it is even a kind of pride to show oneself unwilling to accept the things of God.

To meet this objection it is necessary to refer to what we said in chapters fifteen and sixteen of the second book. There we pointed out that the good that overflows into the soul from supernatural apprehensions is worked in the soul *passively,* without the active operation of any of the faculties. It is therefore unnecessary for the will to perform the act of receiving them. And, as the spirituality deriving from these imaginary apprehensions is given to the soul passively, the soul must remain in a state of passivity with respect to them and must not attach any importance to its internal or external actions. To behave in this manner is to preserve the feelings which come from God. Nor does this stifle the spirit, for the spirit would be stifled only if the soul desired to behave in a manner different from that whereby God is leading it.

Therefore all that the soul must endeavor to do with regard to all the apprehensions which come to it from above is to take care to retain the love which they cause in the interiority of the soul. And only to this effect may the soul at times recall those images and apprehensions which were the cause of its love. For, when the soul does recall them, its love is renewed, the mind is lifted up to God, and the soul has now, as it were, a veritable mine of blessings within itself.

CHAPTER XIV

The spiritual knowledge present in the memory may be either of creatures or of uncreated perfections.

We listed *spiritual knowledge* third among the several types of apprehensions of the memory. It, too, is made present in spiritual memory and reminiscence, and after the soul has experienced one of these apprehensions it can recall it whenever it wishes, by means of the form that was impressed upon it as a kind of spiritual or formal image.

The nature of this knowledge and the manner in which the soul must react to it in order to attain to union with God, have been sufficiently described in chapter twenty-four of the second book. And we said there that these apprehensions of the understanding are of two kinds: they are either apprehensions of uncreated perfections or of creatures. Now these apprehensions may be recalled by the memory, provided they produce good effects; not in order to be retained in the memory but in order that the soul's love and knowledge of God may become more ardent. But if this recollection produces no good effects, they should never be allowed to re-enter the memory. With respect to the knowledge of things uncreated, on the other hand, I say that the soul should try to recall it as often as possible, for this knowledge will then produce certain touches and inner experiences of union with God, and that, after all, is the goal toward which we are aiming to guide the soul.

CHAPTER XV

The general method which the spiritual person must apply with respect to the contents of the memory. Images are good and necessary as means: they serve to remind us of God and the saints.

Before we conclude this discussion of the memory, the spiritual reader should be told something about the method he must invariably follow in order to attain to union with God with respect to this faculty. If the soul is to live in the perfect and pure hope of God, it should never rest in the knowledge of these distinct forms and images, but should immediately turn to God with loving affection and with its memory completely emptied. It must neither think of these things nor give heed to them any more than is necessary for the understanding and fulfillment of its obligations. This means that a man should not refrain from thinking and remembering what he ought to do; for, provided he remains without affection and attachment, this will do him no harm.

But here it should be emphasized that this doctrine of ours has nothing in common with the teachings of those evil men who, impelled by Satanic pride and envy, have been trying to deprive the eyes of the faithful of the holy and necessary use and praiseworthy veneration of images of God and the saints. For we do not teach, as they do, that there should be no such images or that images should not be venerated, but we are rather trying to explain the difference between images and God. And we want men to pass beyond the painted image, so that they may not be impeded thereby from attaining to the living truth, and may not pay more attention to images than is necessary for the attainment of the spiritual. For just as all means are good and necessary for the attainment of an end, so images are necessary as means to remind us of God and the saints. And thus, when we consider a means as more than a mere means and attribute to it a much higher value, it will disturb and hinder us greatly. With respect, then, to the remembrance, veneration, and esteem of images which the Catholic Church places before our eyes, there can be no deception or peril, because we esteem in them only that which they represent; nor does the remembrance of them fail to benefit the soul, since the memory is filled only with the love of that which they represent; and, provided the soul values them no higher than is necessary for this purpose, they will prove an aid to union with God, allowing the soul to soar upward (when God grants it that favor) from the painted image to the living God.

CHAPTER XVI

The dark night of the will. The four affections or passions of the will are: joy, hope, grief, and fear.

We should have accomplished nothing by the purging of the *understanding* (in order to ground it in the virtue of *faith*), and by the purging of the *memory* (in order to ground it in the virute of *hope*), if we purged not the *will* also, so that it may be grounded in the third [theological] virtue, which is *love* and which causes the works that are done in faith to live and be of great value; for without love they are worth nothing. As St. James says: Without the works of love, faith is dead (cf. James 2:20).

And now that we have to treat of the active denudation and night of this faculty, I find no more fitting authoritative testimony than what is written in Deuteronomy, where Moses says: "You must love the Lord your God with the love of your whole heart, and your whole soul, and your whole strength" (Deut. 6:5). In these words is contained all that the spiritual man ought to do, and all that I have here to teach him, so that he may truly attain to God, through union of will, by means of love.

The strength of the soul consists in its faculties, passions, and desires, and all these faculties are governed by the will. Now when these faculties, passions, and desires are oriented by the will toward God, and turned away from all that is not God, then the strength of the soul is preserved for God, and thus the soul is able to love God with its whole strength. And in order to make it possible for the soul to do this, we shall here treat of the purgations of the will from all its unruly inclinations, since it is from these that arise unruly desires, affections, and works. These affective inclinations or passions are four in number, namely: joy, hope, grief, and fear. When these passions are duly ordered by reason and oriented toward God, so that the soul rejoices only in that which serves purely the honor and glory of God, hopes and grieves for nothing else, and fears nothing but God, it is evident that the entire strength and capacity of the soul are being maintained for God and directed toward Him. For, in order to attain to union with God, the thing that is of greatest import is the purging of the will from its affections and desires, because this is the only way whereby a base, human will may become a Divine will, being made one with the will of God.

Now the more strongly these four passions rule in the soul and assail it, the less strongly the soul is attached to God and the greater becomes its dependence on creatures. And from these affections, when they are unrestrained, arise all the vices and imperfections of the soul; and from them, too, arise all of the soul's virtues, when these affections are duly ordered and composed. Moreover, if one of these passions is subjected to the law and order of reason, the others will be ruled and ordered likewise; for they are closely and intimately linked with one another, so that the actual direction of the one becomes the virtual direction of the others. Where your hope is, there will be your joy, your fear, and your grief also. Remember, therefore, that wherever one of these passions is, thither will go the whole soul, the will, and the other faculties, and they will all live as captives of this one passion; and they will then afflict the soul and prevent it from flying upward to the freedom and rest of sweet contemplation and union.

CHAPTER XVII

The first affection of the will: joy.

The first of the passions of the soul and affections of the will is *Joy,* which is a satisfaction of the will, combined with an esteem of something which the will finds desirable. This we say with reference to *active* joy, which is felt when the soul clearly and distinctly understands the cause of its rejoicing, and when the soul has it in its power to rejoice or not. There is another kind of joy which is *passive;* here the will may find itself rejoicing without understanding clearly and distinctly the cause of its joy, and in this case it is not in the soul's power to rejoice or not. Of this passive joy we shall speak later.

Joy may arise from *six* kinds of things or goods: *temporal, natural, sensory, moral, supernatural,* and *spiritual.* These we shall discuss in their order, but before we do so it is necessary to mention one basic presupposition: the will must never rejoice save in that which serves the honor and glory of God; and the greatest honor we can offer Him is that of serving Him according to the counsels of evangelical pefection. Anything that has nothing to do with this objective is of no value and benefit to man.

CHAPTER XVIII

Joy with respect to temporal goods.

The first kind of goods which we have mentioned are *temporal*. And by temporal goods we here understand riches, high rank and offices, and other objects of human aspiration; also children, relatives, marriages, and so on; in all of these the will may find cause for rejoicing. And yet it is clear how vain it is for man to rejoice in riches, titles, rank and position, and in similar objects of human ambition; for a man ought to rejoice in riches only if by being rich he would become a better servant of God; but, as a matter of fact, riches may rather be a cause of giving offense to God. For though it is true that temporal possessions do not necessarily in themselves cause sin, yet the heart of man as a rule clings to them and thus fails God, owing to the frailty of its affections. This is why Our Lord tells us in the Gospel how hard it will be for those who have riches to enter the Kingdom of Heaven—that is, for those who rejoice in their riches (cf. Matt. 19:23; Luke 18:24).

Solomon, who had possessed great riches and knew well their worth, came to say in the end that all things beneath the sun are but vanity, affliction of the spirit, and futile anxiety of the mind (cf. Eccles. 1:14). This we see also in the Gospel, where the man who rejoiced because he had gathered the fruits of many years, was told: You fool, this night you must render your soul and give account; and who will be the master of what you have gathered? (Luke 12:20).

It is vain, then, to rejoice in any of these temporal goods unless a man feels that he can serve God better because of them and that they aid him in making the way to eternal life more secure. For, as Our Lord says: Though a man gain the whole world, he may yet lose his soul (cf. Matt. 16:26). This He said to make us understand that we must not set our joy on anything that is not conducive to the service of God.

CHAPTER XIX

The evils that may befall the soul which sets its joy on temporal goods have their root in the soul's separation from God.

If we had to describe all the evils which engulf the soul when it sets the affections of its will on temporal goods, paper and ink would not suffice and our time would be too short. But they all have their root and origin in one main privative evil, namely, in the soul's separation from God.

This privative evil has four degrees, each one worse than the other. They are well indicated by Moses when he says: "The beloved [people] grew fat and rebellious; pampered, sated, and swollen with pride, they forsook God their Maker and became estranged from God their deliverer" (Deut. 32:15). This "growing fat" of the soul means its becoming engulfed in the enjoyment of creatures. And from this derives the first degree of this evil: the soul's going backward or a blunting of the mind with regard to God. For by setting its joy on any [temporal] thing, and by giving rein to the desire for foolish things, the spiritual person becomes blind with regard to God, and his judgment becomes clouded.

The second degree of this privative evil derives from the first, which is indicated in the words following the passage quoted above: "they were pampered, sated, and swollen with pride." This second degree causes the soul to turn away from the things of God and from holy practices: it no longer finds pleasure in them because it takes pleasure in other things. And those who are in this condition not only have their judgment and understanding darkened with respect to the knowledge of truth and justice, but they also become very slack, tepid, and careless in their efforts to gain such knowledge and to apply it in their works. Because their will is being more and more set aflame with the love of creatures, they fulfill their duties as a mere formality, or because of external compulsion, or by force of habit, rather than because they love to do what they ought to do.

The third degree of this privative evil consists in a complete withdrawal from God and a total indifference with regard to the fulfillment of His law, in order not to lose the enjoyment of worldly things and goods. Their sensual desires cause these persons to relapse into mortal sins. And this third degree is described in the words following the passage quoted above, which are: "They forsook God their Maker." Persons in this condition become very forgetful and dull with respect to everything that has to do with their salvation, but they are all the more zealous and shrewd with respect to the things of the world, in wealth and business deals, etc. Possessed by avarice, they have expanded and dispersed their desire and joy in things created to such a degree that they can never be satisfied: their desire and thirst grow in proportion as they are farther and farther separated from God, the only source that could satisfy them.

The fourth degree of this privative evil is indicated in the last words of our passage, which read: "They have become estranged from God their deliverer." The soul of the covetous is far removed from God, as far as his memory, understanding, and will are concerned: he forgets God as though He were not his God, owing to the fact that he has fashioned for himself a god of mammon and of temporal possessions. These persons do not hesitate to subordinate Divine and supernatural things to temporal things, whereas they ought to do the very opposite, namely, subordinate all temporal things to God, as reason commands. And there are many in this day and age who belong to this category. They are not servants of God, but of mammon, and they are making money their supreme deity and ultimate end.

To this last group belong also those miserable souls who

are so enamored with their possessions that they regard them as their god and are even willing to sacrifice their lives for them. Not infrequently they are giving themselves over to despair and even commit suicide for such miserable ends, thus demonstrating by their acts how wretched is the reward which they receive from their god. And those whom he pursues not to this final evil of self-destruction, he condemns to a living death in the self-torture of anxiety and in many other miseries, and no gladness ever enters their hearts. Thus joy, when it makes temporal possessions its final end, drags a man down to these evils. Wherefore, as David says: Do not be disturbed when a man grows rich; that is, envy him not, thinking that he has an advantage over you, for he cannot take anything with him when he dies, and his worldly glory and joy will not follow him to the grave (cf. Ps. 48:17-18).

CHAPTER XX

The benefits deriving from the soul's withdrawal from temporal things are freedom of spirit, tranquillity, and obedience to God.

The spiritual man, then, must see to it with great care that his heart and his joy do not even begin to develop an attachment to temporal things. In this way he will not only free himself from those pestilential evils which we have described in the preceding chapter, but he will acquire freedom of spirit, clarity of mind, rest, tranquillity, peaceful trust in God, a devout will, and obedience to God. Through his detachment from creatures he will find greater joy and solace in them, because he cannot truly enjoy them as long as he looks upon them with possessive attachment. For such an attachment begets an anxiety which, like a chain, fetters the spirit to the earth and permits no true liberality of heart. In his detachment from temporal things the spiritual man will also acquire a clearer view of them, so that he will the better understand their inherent truth. For the spirit that is purged of the clouds and the species of accidents, penetrates to the essential truth and value of things.

This man, then, rejoices in all things—since his joy is not attached to any of them—as if he possessed them all. But the other, who looks upon them as though they were his exclusive property and possession, loses all pleasure in them. The former, not having set his heart on any of them, possesses them all in great freedom (cf. 2 Cor. 6:10), whereas the latter neither has nor possesses anything: it is rather these things which have taken possession of his heart, so that he has become, as it were, a tormented prisoner.

There is yet another very great and important benefit in this detachment from taking pleasure in creatures: it leaves the heart free for God. And this is the indispensable foundation that disposes the soul for all the favors which God will bestow upon it, and He does not grant them without this disposition. These favors, however, are of such a nature that, even from a temporal point of view, for one joy which the soul renounces for love of Him and for the sake of evangelical perfection, He will reward it a hundredfold, even in this life (cf. Matt. 19:29).

CHAPTER XXI

Natural goods are but means to attain to God: it is vanity to rejoice in them.

By *natural goods* we here understand beauty, grace, loveliness, bodily constitution and all other bodily endowments; and also the natural goods of the soul, such as a good mind, discretion, and other things pertaining to reason. There are many who rejoice in all these gifts, to the end that they themselves or those who are dear to them may possess them, without giving thanks to God Who bestows them in order that, because of these gifts, He may be better known and loved. But it is vanity and delusion to rejoice in them [as ends in themselves], as Solomon says in these words: "Deceitful is grace, and vain is beauty; only the woman who fears the Lord will achieve renown" (Prov. 31:30). Here the Wise Man teaches us that a man should rather be fearful because of these natural gifts, since he may be distracted by them from the love of God. The person, therefore, who has such gifts should be cautious and live carefully, lest, by his vain ostentation, he give cause to any man to become alienated in his heart from God. For these graces and gifts of nature are so seductive and perilous, both to him who possesses them and to him who looks upon them, that there is hardly anyone who entirely escapes from binding and entangling his heart in them.

The spiritual man, then, must purge his will and make it blind to this vain joy, remembering that beauty and all other natural gifts are but dust: they come from dust and will return to it; and grace and beauty are but smoke and earthly vapor. And they must be regarded as such by the man who desires to turn his heart to God with joy and gladness, because God is in Himself all beauty and grace in the most eminent degree and infinitely surpasses all creatures.

CHAPTER XXII

The evils which result when the will rejoices in natural goods.

[This chapter describes in minute detail the many spiritual and bodily evils which result when the will rejoices in *natural* goods as though they were ends in themselves. Six principal groups of evils are listed:

(1) vainglory, presumption, pride, and disdain of our fellow-men; (2) complacency, sensual and carnal pleasures; (3) adulation and vain praise; (4) the blunting

of the reason and the spirit; (5) the distraction of the mind that derives from rejoicing in created things; (6) tepidity and weakness of spirit. The concluding paragraph reads as follows:]

Let us end, then, by giving the instruction necessary to counteract these poisonous evils: When your heart feels itself moved by this vain joy in natural goods, remember how futile, perilous, and pernicious it is to rejoice in anything except in the service of God. Consider how great an evil it was for the angels to rejoice and take pleasure in their beauty and natural endowments, since it was this that plunged them into the abyss of sin. Remember, too, how many evils befall men daily owing to this same vanity, and resolve (while there is still time) to employ the remedy which the poet recommends to those who are becoming attached to these things: Make haste and apply the remedy at the outset; for when evil has had time to grow in the heart, it is too late to apply the remedy and the medicine.

CHAPTER XXIII

The benefits which derive from not taking joy in natural goods.

Many are the benefits which the soul receives by withdrawing the heart [i.e., the will] from this kind of joy. For, aside from the fact that it thus disposes itself for the love of God and for the other virtues, it prepares a straight way for its personal humility and for a general love of its neighbors. For, by not attaching itself to anyone in particular, the soul remains free and overt to love them all, in accordance with God's will. If there is yet some attachment in this love, there is still greater attachment to God. For, in this case, the more this love grows, the more grows our love of God; and the greater our love of God, the greater becomes our love for our neighbor.

And there is yet another great benefit in the renunciation of this kind of joy: it produces great tranquillity in the soul, emptying it of distractions, and bringing recollection to the senses. For, by guarding its doors (which are the senses), the soul guards itself and increases its tranquillity and purity. Finally, those who have made progress in the mortification of this kind of joy [will find] that evil things and the knowledge of them can no longer leave an impress on them or stain them with impurity. The renunciation and mortification, therefore, of this kind of joy result in spiritual purity of soul and body, that is, of spirit and sense; and thus the soul gradually acquires an angelical conformity with God, and both soul and body become a worthy temple of the Holy Ghost. And from this follows that generous goodness of soul which is as necessary for the service of God as is the freedom of spirit. With this aid temptations are easily overcome, trials are patiently endured, and the virtues grow and thrive in abundance.

CHAPTER XXIV

The third kind of natural goods in which the will may rejoice: the goods of sense.

The third kind of natural goods in which the will may rejoice are the *goods of sense*. And by goods of sense we here understand everything in this life that can be apprehended by the senses of sight, hearing, smell, taste, and touch as well as by the internal and external bodily senses of the imagination.

Now the senses may receive pleasure and delight either from the spirit—by means of some inward communication which the spirit receives from God—or from external things that are communicated to the senses. And, as has been stated, neither by way of the spirit nor by way of the senses can the sensory part of the soul know God. It would therefore be vain if the will were to rejoice in the pleasure caused by any of these apprehensions; for the power of the will would thereby be prevented from occupying itself with God and from setting its joy on Him alone. This the soul can do perfectly only by purging itself and becoming blind to any joy of this kind.

I said advisedly that it would be vain if the will were to set its joy upon any of these things [as ends in themselves]. But if the will, as soon as it finds pleasure in that which it hears, sees, and does, soars upward to rejoice in God, then this is very good. In this case the pleasure of the will acts as a motive power and gives the will sufficient strength to do this. And when these inclinations become thus the cause of such devotion and prayer, they not only need not be shunned, but the soul may even derive great benefit from them; for there are souls who are strongly motivated by objects of sense to seek God. But much caution must be observed in this matter, and the effects must be carefully considered. For it often happens that spiritual persons indulge in these delights of sense under the pretext of offering prayer and of surrendering themselves to God, but they are doing this in a way that might be called recreation rather than prayer, since it gives more pleasure to themselves than to God.

I should like, therefore, to offer some advice as to how it can be determined whether these delights of the senses are profitable or not. When, for example, a person listens to music, or sees things which please the eye, or scents sweet fragrances, or tastes delicious foods, or feels tender touches —if his thoughts and the affections of his will turn immediately to God, and if his thinking of God gives him more pleasure than the impulse of sense, this is a sign that he is benefited thereby and that this object of sense is an aid to his spirit. In this manner all these things may legitimately be used, for in this case they serve the end for which God created and gave them, namely, that because of these gifts He should be the better loved and known. And we should keep in mind, furthermore, that a person upon whom these things of sense have such a purely spiritual effect has no desire for them. When they are offered to him, his will passes through them and beyond them and is set upon God. He, on the other hand, who feels not this freedom of spirit, but whose will is detained by these things and pleasures of sense and feeds upon them, is greatly harmed by them and must deny himself their use.

Whatever kind of pleasure of sense, then, presents itself to a spiritual person, he must make use of it only as a means to the attainment of God: he must lift up to Him the joy of his soul, so that his rejoicing may be beneficial, salutary, and perfect.

CHAPTER XXV

The evils which result when the will desires to rejoice in the natural goods of sense.

[This chapter explains that all the evils which arise from any enjoyment of temporal goods—as ends in themselves rather than as means to the ultimate end—follow likewise from rejoicing in this disorderly manner in the objects of sense—evils such as the blunting and darkening of reason, tepidity, spiritual dullness, distraction of mind, unruly sensual desires, immodesty, impurity of thought, envy, and so on. Then follows an enumeration and description of the evils which result from taking disorderly pleasure in the objects of the five bodily senses, such as gluttony, drunkenness, anger, discord, lack of neighborly love, bodily disorders and infirmities, discontent, effeminacy, cowardice, restlessness, etc. The power of reasoning is weakened, and "reason becomes as useless as a broken vessel." Finally, there follow an aversion to spiritual exercises and a general slackening of devotion in the use of the sacraments of penance and the Eucharist.]

CHAPTER XXVI

The spiritual and temporal benefits which the soul derives from denying itself the enjoyment of the things of sense.

Very wonderful are the benefits which the soul derives from denying itself this kind of enjoyment. Some of these are spiritual and some temporal.

First of all, the soul is withdrawn from distraction and becomes recollected in God. And the spirituality and virtues which it has acquired are not only preserved but are steadily increased.

Second, that which was sensual becomes spiritual, and that which was animalic becomes rational, so that the soul is in fact journeying from a human to a virtually angelical mode of life: its humanity and temporality are being gradually transformed into divinity and eternity. This is clearly evident from the fact that in proportion as the powers of sense are diminished and weakened, the contrary [spiritual] powers are increased and strengthened. And thus the spirit is perfected in the heavenly and spiritual gifts and blessings of God.

Third, the pleasures and the rejoicing of the will in temporal goods are immeasurably increased; for, as Our Saviour says, these persons "shall receive reward a hundred-fold in this life" (cf. Matt. 19:29). If, then, you deny yourself one joy, the Lord will give you joy a hundredfold in this life, both spiritually and temporally. And, conversely, for one joy that you take in these things of sense, you will receive grief and misery a hundredfold. To him, therefore, who is pure, all things, high or low, become an occasion of greater good and greater purity. And in the man who lives no longer according to sense, all the operations of the senses and faculties are directed to Divine contemplation. Such a man, being pure in heart, finds in all things a knowledge and a message of God.

From what has been said I now deduce the following guiding rule: until a man has habituated his senses to the purgation of the joys of sense, he must needs deny himself all joy and pleasure with respect to these goods, so that he may be able to withdraw his soul from the life of sense.

There is no need to speak at length of the blessings of glory which, in the life to come, result from the renunciation of these joys. For, aside from the fact that the bodily gifts of the life of glory, such as agility and clarity, will be of much greater excellence, there will be an increase in the essential glory of the soul corresponding to the soul's love of God, for Whose sake it has renounced these things of sense.

CHAPTER XXVII

Moral goods—the fourth kind of temporal goods.

The fourth kind of goods wherein the will may find joy are *moral goods*. By this we here understand the virtues and their habits—in so far as these latter are of a moral nature—the practice of any virtue, the performance of works of mercy, the keeping of the law of God, the exercise of the functions of good government, and generally the realization of all good intentions and inclinations.

These moral goods deserve perhaps more than any of the other kinds of good that the will should rejoice in them. For a man may rejoice in his own affairs for one of two reasons, or for both reasons together: either for what they are in themselves, or for the good which they imply and entail as means and instruments. Now moral goods merit a certain measure of joy on the part of him who possesses them, and this for the first reason, that is, for what they are and what they are worth in themselves. For they bring with them peace and tranquillity, and the right and ordered use of reason, and the corresponding actions, so that, humanly speaking, a man cannot have anything better in this life.

Thus, since these virtues deserve, humanly speaking, to be loved and esteemed for their own sakes, a man may well rejoice in the possession of them, and may practise them for what they are in themselves and for the good things which they bring to man in human and temporal form. This is why philosophers, wise men, and many of the rulers in ancient times esteemed and praised them, and endeavored to acquire and practise them; and although they were pagans and looked at these goods only from the temporal point of view, having regard only for the temporal, corporal, and natural blessings which they knew would result from them, they not only obtained by means of them the temporal renown and the benefits which they sought, but, in addition, they obtained from God—Who loves all that is good, even in barbarians and pagans—longer life, higher honor, greater dominion, and peace (as, for example, in the case of the Romans), because they followed the paths of justice in their laws. And so we see that He gave temporal blessings to those who because of their unbelief were incapable of receiving an eternal reward.

The Christian [on the other hand] must not allow his joy to come to a halt in this first stage, but, since he has the light of faith, wherein he hopes for eternal life—and since without this hope nothing pertaining to this life or the next will be of any value to him—he must rejoice solely and above all else in the possession and use of these goods after the second manner, so that by doing these good works for the love of God he will gain eternal life. And thus—in practising his virtues and good habits—he should set his eyes and his joy solely on serving and honoring God. For without this perspective the virtues are of no value whatsoever in the sight of God, as is seen in [the Gospel parable of] the ten virgins, who had all kept their virginity and had done many good works; and yet, because the joy of five of them was not of the second kind—that is, not directed toward God—but rather of the first and futile kind—that is, they rejoiced in their goods works—they were cast out from Heaven without any reward from the Bridegroom. A Christian, then, should not rejoice in the performance of good works and in the practice of good habits but rather in performing and practising them for the love of God alone, without consideration of anything else. He should always remember that the value of his good works, fasts, alms, penances, etc. is not based on their number and excellence, but on the love of God which prompts him to do these things.

CHAPTER XXVIII

Seven kinds of evil which may befall a man who sets the joy of his will upon moral goods and vainly rejoices in his good works.

The principal evils into which a man may fall by taking a vain joy in his good works and habits are seven in number; and they are all very harmful because they are spiritual in nature.

The first evil is vanity, including pride, vainglory, and presumption; for a man cannot rejoice in his works without esteeming them highly; and this leads to boasting and suchlike things, as we are told of the Pharisee in the Gospel, who prayed and congratulated himself before God, boasting about his fasting and his other good works (cf. Luke 18:12).

The second evil is usually linked with the first: it consists in judging others as wicked, imperfect, and inferior to us, by comparing their acts and good works with our own. Some go even so far as to become angry and envious when they see that others are praised, or do more good works, or are more deserving [of praise] than themselves.

The third kind of evil we observe in those who, since they look for pleasure in the good works they perform, do them only when they see that some pleasure and praise will result from them. And thus, as Christ says, they do everything "in order to be seen by men" (Matt. 23:5) and not for the love of God alone.

The fourth evil follows from the third: these persons will have no reward from God, since they have desired to find in this life joy or consolation or honor or the satisfaction of some other kind of selfish interest in the performance of their good works. Of these Our Saviour says that they have already received their reward (cf. Matt. 6:2). Or how else could the actions of certain people be judged, or what else should we think of the memorials they set up in order to perpetuate their name, lineage or authority? Some even go so far as to have their emblems and coats of arms displayed in our churches, as though they wished to exhibit themselves in places where all can admire them on bended knee. Are we not justified in saying of some people that in the good works they perform they are worshipping themselves more than God? This is the sounding of the trumpet, which, as Our Saviour says, is done by vain men (cf. Matt. 6:3).

In order to flee from this evil, men must hide their good works, so that God alone may see them; and they must hide them not only from others, but even from themselves. Nor must they find satisfaction in them, nor esteem them as though they were of some value, nor derive any pleasure from them. This is the spiritual meaning of those words of Our Lord: "Let not your left hand know what your right hand is doing" (Matt. 6:3).

The fifth of these evils is manifest in the fact that such persons make no progress on the road to perfection; for, since they are attached to the pleasure and consolation which they find in their good works, it follows that when such pleasure and consolation are absent they slacken and do not persevere.

The sixth of these evils lies in the fact that such persons commonly deceive themselves, thinking that the things and good works which give them pleasure are better than those which give them none. And yet, as a rule, those works in which a man practises the greatest self-denial are more acceptable and precious in the sight of God than are those in which he finds consolation and which may very easily become an occasion of self-seeking.

The seventh evil derives from the fact that to the extent that a man does not stifle his vain rejoicing in the performance of moral acts, he is incapable of accepting reasonable counsel and instruction in regard to the works he ought to do. For he is fettered by the habit of weakness which he has acquired in performing good works while he was attached to this vain joy. Such a person is greatly weakened in his love of God and of his neighbor; for the self-love which governs him in relation to his good works causes his love [of God] to grow cold.

CHAPTER XXIX

The benefits which result when the soul withdraws its joy from moral goods.

Very great indeed are the benefits which result when the soul entertains no vain desire to set the joy of the will on this kind of goods. In the first place, it is freed from falling into many temptations and deceits of Satan. And it is not surprising at all that the soul should be secretly deceived by the devil in this kind of joy; for, even though it may be immune to his suggestions, the vain rejoicing itself is a delusion, especially when the human heart is inclined to take pride in good works. For is there greater self-deception in anything than in boasting? And from this the soul is freed when it purges itself from this kind of joy.

The second benefit is that the soul performs its good works with more prudent deliberation and with greater perfection; for, because of this passion of joy, the passions of anger and cupidity become so strong that they will not submit to reason, but quite commonly cause a man to become unstable in his intentions and actions. The wise man, therefore, sets his eyes on the substance and intrinsic quality of his work, not upon the joy and pleasure he derives from it. If he does this, he is not beating the air, but finds in his work a stable joy, without any admixture of bitterness.

The third benefit is truly divine; for when vain joy in good works is silenced, the soul becomes poor in spirit, and this is one of the Beatitudes pronounced by the Son of God when He said: "Blessed are the poor in spirit, for theirs is the Kingdom of Heaven" (Matt. 5:3).

The fourth benefit is that the man who denies himself this joy will be meek, humble, and prudent in whatever he does.

The fifth benefit is that such a person becomes pleasing to God and man, and is freed from inordinate desire, gluttony, spiritual sloth, spiritual envy, and from a multitude of other vices.

CHAPTER XXX

Supernatural goods—the fifth kind of goods in which the will may rejoice: gratiae gratis datae.

The time has now come to treat of the fifth kind of goods wherein the soul may rejoice, and these are *supernatural*. And we call supernatural all the gifts and graces given by God, which transcend the natural faculties and virtues and which are known as *gratiae gratis datae* [i.e., graces given to a person for the good of others], such as the gifts of wisdom and knowledge which God gave to Solomon, and the graces of which St. Paul speaks—namely, faith, the gifts of healing, the working of miracles, prophecy, the knowledge and discernment of spirits, the interpretation of words, and the gift of tongues.

Although it is true that these [supernatural] goods are also spiritual, I have thought it best to make a distinction between them, because there is a difference in their object: Whereas *spiritual* graces have to do only with the Creator and the human soul, *supernatural* graces have to do with the creature. Moreover, they differ in substance and consequently in their operation, and for this reason our instruction concerning them must of necessity take into account these differences.

Speaking, then, of supernatural gifts and graces as we here understand them, I say that, in order to purge ourselves of vain joy in them, it is necessary to point out two types of benefits—temporal and spiritual—that derive from this kind of gifts. The temporal benefits consist in the healing of the sick, the restoring of sight to the blind, the raising of the dead, the driving out of devils, the foretelling of the future, and other things of this kind. The spiritual and eternal benefit [deriving from these works] is that God is known and served by him who performs them, or by those in whom or in whose presence they are performed.

With respect to the first kind of benefits—namely, the temporal—supernatural works and miracles deserve little or no rejoicing on the part of the soul; for without the second kind of benefit [namely, the spiritual], they are of little or no importance to man, since they are not in themselves a means for uniting the soul with God. These supernatural works may in fact be performed and these graces obtained by those who are not in the state of grace and love. They may be performed regardless of whether these persons truly give thanks to God and acknowledge Him as their author, or whether they perform them falsely, with the aid of Satan —as did Simon Magus—or by means of other secret natural devices. And St. Paul tells us precisely what these works are worth without the second [spiritual] benefit, when he says: "Though I speak in every tongue of men and of angels, and have not love, I am as tinkling brass or the hollow sound of a bell. And though I had the gift of prophecy and knew the depth of all hidden secrets, and had utter faith so that I could move mountains, but had not love, I would be nothing" (1 Cor. 13:1-2).

A man, then, should rejoice, not when he has such graces and puts them to good use, but when he gains from them the spiritual fruit of serving God with true love, for herein he reaps the fruit of eternal life.

CHAPTER XXXI

The evils which result when the will rejoices in supernatural goods are: deception, loss of faith, vanity.

It seems to me that three principal evils may befall the soul when it sets its joy upon supernatural goods: (1) it may deceive and be deceived; (2) it may suffer the loss of its faith; (3) it may indulge in vainglory or some other kind of vanity.

As to the first of these evils, it is a very easy thing to deceive others and to deceive oneself by taking joy in these supernatural works. And the reason is that, in order to know which of them are false and which are true, and how and at what time they should be performed, much counsel and enlightenment from God are needed, and these are greatly impeded by the joy we take in these works and by the esteem in which we hold them.

And the evil of this joy not only leads men on to make wicked and perverse use of these graces, but even to use them when God is not the giver of them, as happened in the case of those who prophesied according to their own fancies and told about visions which they had invented or which the devil had presented to them. For it is well to remember that all those magicians and pseudo-prophets who lived among the children of Israel and whom Saul destroyed because they had tried to imitate the true prophets of God, had fallen into such abominations and deceits.

Those, therefore, who have such supernatural gifts and graces should restrain their desire to make use of them and should refrain from rejoicing in them; for God, Who bestows these gifts by supernatural means, for the sake of His Church and its members, will also move such persons supernaturally in the proper manner and at the suitable time.

The second evil—namely, the loss of faith—may proceed from the first. And this may come about in two ways: first, with respect to others; for, when such a person sets out to perform a miraculous or mighty work needlessly and at the wrong time, he is not only tempting God, which is a great sin, but he may not even succeed in his undertaking and will thus introduce distrust and contempt of the faith into human hearts. Secondly, faith and its merit may be destroyed within ourselves; for, if we attribute much importance to these miracles, we cease to adhere to the substantial practice of faith, which is a habit that is clothed in darkness; and thus, the greater the number of visible signs and of witnesses, the less merit is there in faith. These miracles are therefore never worked by God unless they are really necessary for faith. This is why Christ reproved the Pharisees, telling them: "Unless you see signs and miracles, you will not believe" (John 4:48). Those, then, who love to rejoice in these supernatural works are greatly weakened in their faith.

The third evil is that men, because of their rejoicing in these works, fall prey to vainglory or some other kind of vanity. For their very rejoicing in these miracles is vanity, unless their joy be purely in God and for God.

CHAPTER XXXII

Two benefits which derive from the renunciation
of rejoicing in supernatural graces are the exaltation
of God and the exaltation of the soul.

Aside from the benefits which the soul gains by being free
of the evils mentioned in the preceding chapter, it derives
two major positive benefits from denying itself this kind of
joy. The first is that it thereby magnifies and exalts God;
and the second is that it exalts itself. For [by this renuncia-
tion] God is exalted in the soul in a twofold manner: first,
by the withdrawal of the heart and the joy of the soul from
everything that is not God, so that they can be set upon Him
alone. And because in this way the soul has its center in
God alone, He is exalted and magnified when He makes
manifest to the soul His eminence and grandeur; for in this
elevation of joy God gives testimony of Himself, revealing
Who He is. And this cannot come to pass unless the will be
emptied of joy and consolation with respect to all things.

The second benefit—whereby the soul itself is exalted
—derives from the withdrawal of the will from all visible
signs and testimonies, so that the soul is uplifted in purest
faith, which God infuses and greatly increases. And simultaneously He increases in the soul the other two theological
virtues, which are love and hope, so that—by means of the
dark and nude habit of faith—the soul rejoices in the highest
Divine knowledge; and by means of the virtue of love it
rejoices in the delights of Divine Love, so that the will no
longer finds joy in anything but the living God; and by
means of the virtue of hope the soul also enjoys full satisfaction in the memory. And all this is a marvellous blessing
and of greatest moment in that it leads essentially and directly to the perfect union of the soul with God.

CHAPTER XXXIII

The sixth kind of goods in which the will may rejoice
are spiritual goods.

Since it is our intention to lead the spirit by means of these
spiritual goods to the Divine union of the soul with God,
and since we have to deal now specifically with this sixth
kind of goods—which are of the greatest service to this end
—it behoves both myself and the reader to consider this
matter with particular care.

By spiritual goods I understand all those which move
and aid the soul on its way to the things of God and which
have a direct bearing on the soul's communion with God.

I begin then by making a distinction between these
highest goods and by saying that there are two kinds of
spiritual goods: the one kind is delectable, the other painful.
And the nature of each of these kinds is likewise twofold:
both the delectable and the painful spiritual goods comprise
clear things that are distinctly understood, and others that
are not understood clearly and distinctly, but are rather dark
and obscure.

Among all these we may again make certain distinctions
with respect to the faculties of the soul. For some spiritual
goods, which are related to the sphere of knowledge, pertain
to the understanding; others, being related to the affections,
pertain to the will; and still others, being of the imaginary
kind, pertain to the memory.

Those spiritual goods which are painful we leave for
later consideration, since they pertain to the *passive night*
[of the soul] and will be discussed in their proper place.
And we leave for later discussion also that delectable kind
which we described as having to do with indistinct and obscure things. At this juncture we shall speak only of those

delectable [spiritual] goods which relate to things that are clear and distinct.

CHAPTER XXXIV

The will, too, must be emptied of rejoicing
in apprehensions.

Since we spoke in the second and third book of the manner in which the faculties of the *memory* and the *understanding* are to conduct themselves with respect to the apprehensions of both these faculties, in order to set them on the road to Divine union, it suffices to say that what has been stated concerning the necessity of emptying these faculties of all kinds of apprehensions, applies equally to the *will:* it must be emptied of all rejoicing in these apprehensions.

CHAPTER XXXV

Spiritual goods which can be distinctly apprehended
by the will. Motivating goods. On the use and abuse
of images.

The kinds of goods which may give joy to the will in a distinct manner can be reduced to four. They are: (1) *motivating goods;* (2) *inciting or persuasive goods;* (3) *directive goods;* (4) *perfective goods.* Of these we shall speak in orderly sequence; and first, of the *motivating* kind, that is, of images and portraits of saints, places of prayer, and religious ceremonies.

Now the *use of images* has been sanctioned by the Church for two main ends, namely that we may venerate in them the saints, and that the will may be moved by them and devotion to the saints may be awakened. When they serve this purpose they are beneficial, and it is necessary to make use of them. To this end we must give preference to those images which most move the will to devotion, and our eyes must be set on this motive rather than on the value and deftness of their workmanship and their decorative appearance; [otherwise] only the senses are pleased and delighted, and the love and rejoicing of the will remain caught in this pleasure of sense; and this wholly thwarts true spirituality, which demands annihilation of the affections with respect to all particular things. Some persons even rejoice in the sight of images to such a degree that their enjoyment amounts to idolatry.

The truly devout person sets his devotion primarily on that which is invisible; he needs and uses few images, and he gives preference to those which are in harmony with the Divine rather than with the human. And his heart is not attached to the images he uses; for, if he is left without them, he feels little distress, since he seeks within himself the living image, which is Christ crucified, for Whom he would rather forsake all and be left with nothing at all. He remains in deep quiet, even when all the motives and means which lead him closer to God are taken from him.

Let the soul rest assured that the more closely it is attached to an image or a motive, the less will its devotion and prayer ascend to God. We should use, then, these instruments only as an aid to devotion; and yet, because of our imperfection, they may hinder our spiritual progress, no less so than our selfish attachment to anything else.

Our vain and inordinate desires are of such a nature and intensity that they try to cling to everything. For what else is, for example, your desire to own an artfully fashioned rosary but an attachment of your joy to a mere instrument [of devotion]? This is not different from giving preference to one image rather than to another, considering not whether it will awaken greater Divine love within you but rather whether it is more precious or more deftly made. If you were employing your desire and your joy solely in loving God, you would remain totally indifferent to any such considerations.

CHAPTER XXXVI

Continuation of the discussion on images.
On pilgrimages.

A great deal might be said about the stupidity which many people exhibit with regard to images. Their foolishness often goes so far that they place more confidence in some images than in others, in the belief that God will listen to them more willingly when they venerate these rather than those, even though they represent the same thing, as when there are, for example, two pictures of Christ or two pictures of Our Lady. This attitude reveals a very crude conception of man's communication with God and of the kind of devotion and honor we owe Him, since all that matters is the faith and the purity of heart of the person who prays. For if God sometimes grants more favors by means of one image than by another of the same kind, this is not because the one is in itself more efficacious than the other, but because some persons awaken their devotion better by means of one rather than another. If they had the same intensity of devotion with respect to the one as with respect to the other, they would receive the same favors from God (even if they were left without any images). For God surely [grants these favors] not because of the image, which as such is only a painted picture, but because of the devotion and faith which a person feels with respect to the saint whom the image represents.

Our Lord often grants these favors by means of images which are located at secluded and solitary places. One reason for this is that the resolution and effort required to journey to these places tend to increase the intensity of the affective devotion and prayer. Another reason is that we thus withdraw from noise and from people, so that in our prayer we may follow the example of Our Lord. Wherefore, a person who makes a pilgrimage does well if he sets out at a time when no other people are doing the same. For I should never advise anyone to make a pilgrimage in a big crowd, because, as a rule, people return from these occasions much more distracted than they were prior to their departure. And many make these pilgrimages for recreation rather than for devotion. And thus, in short, when there is devotion and faith, any image will suffice; but if there is no devotion and faith, none will suffice. Our Saviour was indeed a very living image in the world; and yet those who had no faith, even though they walked at His side and witnessed His miracles, derived no benefit from them.

CHAPTER XXXVII

An image must direct the rejoicing of the will toward God.

Just as images—when used in the proper way—are of great benefit for remembering God and the saints, and for moving the will to devotion, so they will lead into great error if—especially when supernatural phenomena occur in connection with them—the soul is not able to conduct itself in a way that is fitting for its journey to God. Let the devout person, then, take care that, when he sees such an image, he allow not his senses to be absorbed by it—whether it be corporeal or imaginary, whether it be beautifully made or richly adorned, whether the devotion it awakens be of sense or of spirit, and whether it be connected with supernatural phenomena or not. The soul must pay no heed whatever to these accidental matters, but must raise its spirit from the image to that which it represents; for the thing of sense or the painted object cannot serve as substitutes for the living reality and the spirit.

CHAPTER XXXVIII

On places of prayer and of worship.

Some persons never tire of adding images of one kind or another to their oratories, and they take great pleasure in the order and arrangement in which they place them. Yet they do not love God more because of this—they rather love Him less, since the pleasure which they find in these painted adornments is withheld, as we have pointed out, from the living reality. When your senses are absorbed by these things in such a way that your heart is greatly hindered in its journey to God, He will not only fail to reward you, but He will even chastise you for not having sought His pleasure in all things rather than your own. Of this you can find clear evidence in the description of that festival in which the people indulged on the occasion of His Majesty's entry into Jerusalem. They received Him with songs and with branches, and Our Lord wept (cf. Matt. 21:9); for their hearts were far removed from Him, and they paid homage to Him only by these external signs and expressions. We may even say that they were making a festival for themselves rather than for God. And the same is done by many in our time; for, when there is some solemn festival, the people are merry because of the pleasure they themselves find in it rather than in order to please God. They often regard such a feast as an occasion for seeing or being seen, or for eating, or for some other selfish end. How many festivals, oh my God, are celebrated in Your name by the sons of men in which the devil has a greater share than You! And how often will You say on these occasions: "This people honors Me with its lips, but its heart is far from Me" (Matt. 15:8). And thus to serve Him for any other reason than solely because He is Who He is, is to serve Him without regard for Him as the ultimate cause and end.

CHAPTER XXXIX

On the proper use of churches and other
places of prayer.

In order that the spirit may be guided by God by means of this kind of spiritual goods, it is well to point out that it is permissible and even expedient for beginners to find some sensory sweetness and pleasure in certain images, places of prayer, and other visible objects of devotion, inasmuch as these persons have not yet weaned or detached their desire from the things of the world, so that they are prepared to abandon the one pleasure for the other. But the spiritual person who wants to make progress must strip himself of all those pleasures and desires wherein the will may rejoice. And so, although he may make use of images and special places of prayer for a while, his spirit will soon come to rest in God, and he will forget all things of sense.

Therefore, though it is better to pray where there is more propriety, one should nonetheless give preference to a place where sense and spirit are least hindered on their road to God. In this respect we should pay heed to what Our Saviour replied to the Samaritan woman, when she asked Him which was a more fitting place to pray, the temple or the mountain. He answered that true prayer was not connected with either the mountain or the temple, but that those worshippers with whom the Father is well pleased must adore Him in spirit and in truth (cf. John 4:23-24). Wherefore, although churches and attractive sites are properly equipped for prayer, yet, for so intimate a matter as personal communion with God, one should choose a place which gives sense the least occupation and foothold. It is therefore commendable to give preference to a place that is solitary and austere, so that the spirit may rise to God wholly and directly, without being hindered or detained by visible things. Our Saviour always chose solitary places for prayer, in order to give us an example.

CHAPTER XL

The inward recollection of the spirit.

The reason, then, why some spiritual persons never enter wholly into the true joys of the spirit is that they never succeed in actually raising their desire for rejoicing above these external and visible things. In order, then, to purge the will from vain joy and futile desire, and to direct it to God in your prayer, your only consideration must be that your conscience is pure, your will wholly rapt in God, and your mind truly set upon Him.

CHAPTER XLI

[This chapter treats of certain internal and external evils which may befall persons who take pleasure in objects of sense and who are looking for gratification of the senses when they attend places of devotion. They find it impossible to dispose themselves for prayer unless the place suits their personal taste. This attitude leads to instability and restlessness, and prevents spiritual recollection.]

CHAPTER XLII

[This chapter speaks of three different kinds of places of devotion. The discussion of the first kind deals with specific locations which may either help or hinder spiritual recollection and tranquillity of mind. Reference is made to the modest and austere places chosen by the anchorites and other holy hermits and to the monastic foundation of St. Benedict. The second kind relates to places where God is wont to grant certain special spiritual graces. "It is good to pray at such places occasionally, provided the desire is free from attachment." The examples cited refer specifically to the place where God appeared to Abraham and where Abraham built an altar (cf. Gen. 12:8; 13:4), to the place where God appeared to Jacob (Gen. 28:13-19), "who erected there a stone and anointed it with oil"; and to the place where the angel appeared to Hagar (cf. Gen. 16:16). The third kind has to do with special places where God manifests Himself for specific purposes, such as Mount Sinai, "where He gave the Ten Commandments to Moses" (cf. Exod. 24:12), or Mount Horeb, "where He appeared to our father Elias" (3 Kings 19:8).]

The reason why God chooses these places rather than others is known to Him alone. But it behoves us to know that all this is for our own good. He will hear our prayers in these places, but also at any other place, wherever we pray to Him in perfect faith.

CHAPTER XLIII

Other motives for prayer: ceremonies.

[This chapter deals critically with various ceremonies, some of which are of a purely external nature and at times border on superstitious practices. They have to be used with caution and discrimination if they have no essential relation to the central substance of communal liturgical worship and individual prayer.]

CHAPTER XLIV

Devotions and ceremonies should serve only one purpose: they must lead the joy and the strength of the will to God.

Devout persons, then, should realize that the more they rely on these [external] things and ceremonies, the less confidence they have in God. There are people who multiply their petitions in order to obtain a certain thing, when it would be better to pray for things of much greater importance for them, such as a true cleansing of their consciences and a deeper understanding of matters that concern their salvation. In this way they would obtain that which is most important for them and, in addition, all other things that are good for them (although they might not have prayed for them). For this is precisely what Our Lord promised when He said: "Make it your first and principal care to find the Kingdom of God and His approval, and all these other things shall be yours without the asking" (Matt. 6:33).

And, as far as various ceremonies connected with prayer and devotion are concerned, we should not set our will upon other ceremonies and forms of prayer than those which Christ and His Church have taught us. And all He taught [His disciples] was the seven petitions of the *Pater Noster,* wherein are included all our spiritual and temporal needs; and He did not teach them many other kinds of verbal prayer and ceremonial. On the contrary, He told them that when they prayed they should not desire to use many words, since our heavenly Father knows well what our needs are (cf. Luke 11:1-2; Matt. 6:7-8). He exhorted them only—but this most earnestly—to persevere in prayer; and on another occasion He told them that they ought to pray continually and never weaken in their prayer (cf. Luke 18:1). And the ceremonies He taught us to use in our prayers are only two in number: we should pray either in the secrecy of our chamber, where, without being disturbed by noise and without being distracted by anyone, we can pray with a pure heart and with our whole mind (cf. Matt. 6:6); or else, we should follow His example and go to a solitary and deserted place, preferably in the great stillness of the night. And thus there is no reason why we should set any limit of time, or confine our prayers to any special days or hours; nor is there any reason to use other forms in our words and prayers than those which the Church uses and which all can be reduced to those which we have described as being implied in the petitions of the *Pater Noster*.

CHAPTER XLV

The second kind of distinct [spiritual] goods in which the will may vainly rejoice: inciting or persuasive goods.—On preaching and preachers.

The second kind of distinct delectable goods wherein the will may vainly rejoice has to do with those which incite or persuade us to serve God and which we have therefore called *inciting* or *persuasive goods*. This kind of good is connected with preaching and preachers, and we shall consider two aspects of this matter, the one relating to the preachers themselves, and the other relating to those who listen to their sermons.

As to the first aspect, it must be pointed out that the essential function of preaching is spiritual rather than vocal. For, although preaching is practised by means of the spoken word, its power and efficiency lie not in the letter but in the inward spirit. Wherefore, however lofty be the doctrine that is preached, and however finished the rhetoric and style in which the preaching is clothed, it brings as a rule no more benefit than that which is conveyed by the spirituality that is embodied in the preacher.

To the end that the force of the preacher's sermon bear fruit in the hearer, both the preacher and the hearer must be properly disposed. As a rule, however, the benefit that is derived from any instruction depends on the [moral and spiritual] disposition of the teacher. And Our Lord is provoked to anger by those who, though they are teaching the law of God, do not practise what they teach, and who, while they preach spirituality, do not possess it themselves. This is why God tells us through the mouth of St. Paul: You are teaching others, but you have failed to teach yourselves (cf. Rom. 2:21).

We know from common observation that the better the life of the preacher, the greater is the fruit of his preaching, however unpolished his style may be, however unfinished his rhetorical art, and however commonplace his instruction. For though it is true that a good style, catching gestures, sublime doctrinal instruction, and eloquence are very effective motivating forces when they are accompanied by true spirituality, it is equally true that without such spirituality very little or nothing of the spiritual substance of a sermon remains in the will, no matter how much pleasure and delight the preaching may give to the sense and the understanding. As a rule, in this case, the will remains as weak and indolent with regard to good works as it was before. Although marvellous things may have been marvellously said by the preacher, they serve only to delight the ear, like a concert of music or the pealing of bells. This teaching of ours finds support in what St. Paul told the Corinthians when he said: "When I came to you, brethren, and preached Christ's message to you, I did so without any sublimity of philosophic doctrine; and my words and preaching depended not on the eloquence devised by human wisdom, but rather on the testimony I gave of the spirit and the truth" (1 Cor. 2:1-4).

[This chapter concludes the *ASCENT TO MOUNT CARMEL*. The treatise is incomplete, and so is this chapter on preaching and preachers: the discussion of the proper disposition of the hearer as well as the discussion of the last two divisions mentioned in chapter thirty-five—concerning *directive* and *perfective* spiritual goods—are missing].

PART II
THE PASSIVE NIGHT OF THE SOUL

BOOK ONE

The Night of Sense

THE FIRST STANZA

In a dark night,
My heart aglow with love,
—Oh, blessed lot!—
I went forth unseen
From my house that was at last in deepest rest.

Exposition of the passive night.

In this first stanza the soul relates how it went forth from self-love and from its selfish affection for all things, and how it died to them all and to itself, in order to attain to the sweet and blissful life in God. It says that this going forth from itself and from all things was a "dark night." The soul here refers to the purgative light of *contemplation* which causes this denial of self and of all things in a *passive* manner. And the soul stresses the great happiness with which it was so abundantly favored on its way to God through this night that none of its three enemies—the world, the devil, and the flesh—could hinder it. For this night of purgative contemplation had put to sleep and deadened, in the house of the soul's sensuality, all unruly and inordinate passions and desires. And for this reason the soul begins its song with the words, "in a dark night."

CHAPTER I

The imperfections of beginners.

Into this dark night souls are being gradually introduced when God leads them from the state of beginners—who are

162   THE PASSIVE NIGHT OF THE SOUL

still walking on the spiritual road of *meditation*—to the state
of those more advanced in the spiritual life, who have already entered the state of *contemplation*. And after they
have passed through the state of contemplation, He raises
them even further to the state of *perfection,* which is that
of the supernatural union with God.

Now in order to gain a better understanding of the
nature of this night of the soul and of the reason why God
leads the soul into it, we must first of all mention certain
peculiarities of beginners, so that they may recognize the
weaknesses of the state in which they are and may take
courage and awaken in themselves the desire that God will
lead them into this night. For in this night the soul gains
strength and firmness in its virtues and thus prepares itself
for the unspeakable delights of the love of God.

As soon as the soul turns to the service of God with
firm determination, He begins, as a rule, to nurture and
caress it spiritually, as a loving mother nurtures and caresses her tender child. But as the child grows bigger, the
mother gradually withholds her caresses and hides her tender
love. She no longer carries the child in her arms but allows
it to stand and walk on its own feet. And the grace of God
acts like such a loving mother.

Souls [which are spiritually reborn by their new warmth
and fervor in the service of God] often find delight in spending long periods of time in prayer; they take pleasure in
penances, rejoice in fasts, and find consolation in the reception of the sacraments and in spiritual conversation. But
such persons frequently show nevertheless many spiritual
weaknesses and imperfections. For they are often moved
to indulge in these spiritual exercises and devotional practices by the consolation and pleasure they find in them.

In order that it may be seen more clearly how weak
these beginners still are in the practice of the virtues, and
how they do with ease only that which gives them this kind
of pleasure, we shall describe their actions with reference

to the seven *capital sins,* and we shall indicate some of their many imperfections in relation to each of these sins.

CHAPTER II

Imperfections of beginners: spiritual pride.

When these beginners feel that they have become very fervent and diligent in spiritual things and in devout exercises, there often awakens in them a certain kind of secret pride, and they succumb to the temptation of being well satisfied with their works and with themselves. And this is followed by a very vain desire to speak of spiritual things in the presence of others. They would rather teach others than learn from them, and they condemn others in their heart when they see that they do not practise the kind of devotion which they themselves regard as exemplary. Some of these persons even go so far astray that they want none to be judged virtuous but themselves. They see the speck of dust in their brother's eye but are unaware of the beam in their own (cf. Matt. 7:3). They use a strainer to find a gnat [in the food of others], and they themselves swallow a camel (cf. Matt. 23:24).

As these persons think too highly of themselves, they are filled with good intentions but accomplish very little. Sometimes they are anxious that others should see how spiritual and devout they are, and to this end they occasionally draw attention to themselves by gestures, sighs, and other conspicuous demonstrations. When they are in rapture or fall into ecstacies, it usually happens in public rather than in secret.

Some of these souls worry little about their faults, except at certain times when they are suddenly overwhelmed with sadness at seeing themselves so weak: they believed themselves to be saints, and now they become very angry and impatient with themselves; and this is another imperfection. Often they turn to God with great anxiety, asking Him to take from them their imperfections and faults, but they do this motivated by the desire to live in peace and free from trouble, rather than for God's sake.

Those, on the other hand, who at this stage are going on to perfection proceed in a different manner and with a different frame of mind. They make progress in humility and give an edifying example; they think nothing of their own works and are not satisfied with themselves, while at the same time they consider all others far better. And as they have such a low opinion of themselves, they want others to think of them in like manner. They desire to be despised and that their works should be held in no esteem. And they think it very strange that anyone should say good things of them. These are all signs of a spirit that is simple, pure, sincere, and very pleasing to God.

CHAPTER III

Spiritual avarice.

Many of these beginners show at times also great spiritual avarice. One hardly ever finds them satisfied with the kind of spirituality which God gives them. They are very disconsolate and discontented because they do not find in spiritual things the kind of consolation which they seek. Many can never get enough of spiritual counsel and instruction, and they acquire and read many books which treat of these matters, spending much more time with their perusal than they do in practising the much needed self-denial and in working on the perfection of the inward poverty of the spirit. They burden themselves with curious and costly images, rosaries, and crucifixes, and others you may see adorned with medals, amulets, and relics, like children with their toys. What I condemn in all these practices is the attachment of the heart and the affection these persons have for the shape, the number, and the external appearance of these things, because this attitude is contrary to that poverty of spirit which solely considers the substance of devotion. For true devotion must issue from the heart and must have regard only for the truth and essence of what these things represent.

Those, therefore, who proceed on the road of beginners in the right manner, do not attach themselves to such visible aids, nor do they burden themselves with them. They have only one concern and desire: to be pleasing and acceptable to God. And they generously surrender all their spiritual and temporal goods and take great delight in relinquishing all for the sake of God and out of love for their neighbor.

From these and from all other imperfections the soul cannot be perfectly cleansed until God places it into the passive purgation of this dark night. But the soul, on its part, must, as far as it can, try to purify and perfect itself, so that it may become worthy of being taken by God into His Divine care, in which He heals the soul of all imperfections which it was unable to cure by its own efforts.

CHAPTER IV

Spiritual impurity.

With respect to the sin of impurity, beginners have many imperfections, which might be called *spiritual impurities*. It often happens that there arise in the sensual part of the soul impure impulses and acts (which the soul is powerless to prevent), at the very time when the soul is engaged in spiritual exercises, or on the occasion of the reception of the sacraments of penance and holy communion. These involuntary impulses proceed from one of the following three causes:

The first cause is often the intensity of the joy which human nature takes in spiritual things. The spirit, which is the higher part of human nature, is then moved to joy and delight in God, while the lower sensual part is moved to sensual pleasure and delight. And thus it may happen that the soul is deeply rapt in prayer according to the spirit and simultaneously experiences and suffers passively and with revulsion rebellious sensual impulses in its sensual part. But once the sensual part has been transformed by the purgation of the dark night, it no longer has these weaknesses; for then it is no longer the sensual part which receives the Divine Spirit, but the sensual part is itself drawn into the spirit.

The second cause from which these rebellious impulses sometimes proceed is the devil, who, in order to disquiet and upset the soul, stirs up in its nature these motions of impurity. And in persons who are inclined to melancholy these impulses are sometimes so powerful that one must greatly pity them because of their great suffering. Persons who are subject to such attacks are as a rule not freed from them until they are cured from their melancholy or until their soul has entered into the dark night.

The third cause of these impure impulses and of the struggle they cause in the soul is often the fear which such persons have of these movements of their thoughts. And some souls are of such a sensitive and excitable nature that, as soon as they experience in their prayer some spiritual joy, the spirit of impurity begins to stir. The reason for this is that any nervous excitement upsets their natural disposition and raises their blood pressure. And the same thing happens when they become angry or suffer from any other emotional disturbance.

Our Lord says in the Gospel: "What is born of the flesh is flesh, and what is born of the spirit is spirit" (John 3:6). This means that the love which is born of sensuality remains caught in the sensual, and the love which is born of the spirit is directed to the spirit of God and causes spirituality to grow. By this difference we can recognize these two kinds of love. And when the soul enters into the dark night, it brings order into these two loves: the love for God is strengthened and purified, and sensual love is deprived of its strength and mortified.

CHAPTER V

The sin of anger.

Since many beginners have an inordinate desire for the joys of the spirit, their experience of these joys often leads them into many imperfections that have their source in the *sin of anger*. As soon as they are deprived of the taste and enjoyment of spiritual things, they naturally feel very discontented. They are easily irritated at mere trifles and become sometimes quite unbearable. Now as long as this discontent is not allowed to become predominant, it is not sinful but merely an imperfection of which the soul must be purged by the aridity and the trials of the dark night.

Other spiritual persons become irritated and overly zealous in watching and judging the faults of others. They act as if they themselves were accomplished masters of virtue. All this, of course, is contrary to the spirit of meekness.

Others again become indignant and highly impatient with themselves when they observe their own imperfection. And this great impatience derives from their ambition to become saints in one single day. Many of them have good intentions and make grand resolutions, but they are not humble and place too much confidence in themselves. And the more resolutions they make, the more often they fall and the greater becomes their annoyance with themselves, since they do not have the patience to wait for that which

God will give them when it pleases Him. This, too, is contrary to the spirit of meekness. And all this can be wholly remedied only by the purgation of the dark night.

CHAPTER VI

The sin of spiritual gluttony.

Numerous are the imperfections of beginners with respect to *spiritual gluttony,* the fourth capital sin. Allured by the sweetness and pleasure which beginners find in their spiritual exercises, they are apt to strive more for refreshment of the spirit than for purity and true devotion. And their spiritual gluttony drives them to extremes and causes them to go beyond the limits of that moderation in which alone the virtues endure and prosper. Some ruin themselves by excessive penances, while others weaken themselves with fasts and by doing more than their frailty can endure, paying no heed to the needs and requirements of their bodies. They are persons devoid of reason and common sense, who have a higher regard for penances than for humility and obedience. And inasmuch as all extremes are reprehensible, and as in behaving in this manner such persons follow only the dictates of their own will, they grow in depravity rather than in virtue. Some become indeed so miserable that they lose all desire to perform these devotional exercises. And if they are told [by their spiritual directors] to renounce their stubborn self-will and to subject themselves to the will of God, they become the prey of sadness, laxity, and tepidity.

When such persons receive holy communion, they are more interested in experiencing a feeling of sweetness than in humbly revering and praising the inward presence of God. They do not understand that the sensory experience is the least of the blessings which are worked by the reception of this Most Holy Sacrament and that the invisible grace which it bestows is of much greater importance. All this reveals great imperfection and is a great offence against the majesty of God, Who demands a pure faith.

In a similar manner these persons behave in the practice of prayer. They believe that in prayer everything depends on experiencing sensible pleasure and devotion, and by trying to obtain this by hook or by crook they exhaust their strength and weary their heads. And when they do not succeed in finding this pleasure, they become disconsolate and think they have accomplished nothing. They try one kind of meditation after another, always hunting, as it were, for the attainment of this kind of pleasure in the things of God. But God, in His great justice, wisdom, and love, denies it to them; for, if He were to do otherwise, this spiritual gluttony and inordinate desire would become the source of countless evils. This is why it is necessary for such persons to enter into the dark night, so that they may be purged from this childishness.

In conclusion, I should like to say that spiritual sobriety and moderation lead to an entirely different temper, which manifests itself in mortification, fear [of God], and humble submission in all things. And this spiritual sobriety will also make us realize that the perfection and the value of things consist not in the number of our works or in the pleasure we derive from them, but in our ability to deny ourselves in performing them.

CHAPTER VII

The sins of spiritual envy and sloth.

Beginners have also many imperfections with respect to the two remaining capital sins, which are *spiritual envy* and *sloth*. As far as envy is concerned, many experience displeasure when they see others in the possession of spiritual goods. They feel sensibly hurt because others surpass them on this road, and they resent it when others are praised. This, however, is quite contrary to love, which, as St. Paul says, rejoices in goodness (cf. 1 Cor. 13:6). And if love has any envy, it is a holy envy; for love grieves at not possessing the virtues of others, but it rejoices that another person possesses them, and it is greatly pleased when others surpass us in the service of God.

As to spiritual sloth, many beginners shy away and flee from things of a spiritual nature because they do not appeal to their sensible taste. For, as they have found much sweetness in spiritual things, they are wearied by things in which they find no such sweetness. Since they want to have completely their own way in spiritual things and insist on following the inclination of their will, it is with a dejected spirit and with great repugnance that they enter upon the narrow way, which, as Christ says, is the way of life (cf. Matt. 7:14).

The enumeration of these imperfections may suffice for our present purpose, although they are but a few among the many that are encountered in this first stage of the spiritual life of beginners. It all goes to show how necessary it is that God places them in the state of progressives. And this He does by introducing them into the dark night of which we are now going to speak. May God give me His Divine light, so that I may be able to speak about this matter in a way that is profitable to souls. For such Divine illumination is greatly needed in so difficult an undertaking.

CHAPTER VIII

"In a dark night"
The beginning of the explanation of this
"dark night": night of sense and night of spirit.

This night of contemplation produces in spiritual persons two kinds of darkness or purgation, corresponding to the sensual and the spiritual part of man's nature. The first night—or the purgation of sense—subjects the sense to the spirit. The second night—or the purgation of the spirit—prepares and disposes the soul for the union of love with God. While the night of sense is fairly common and is experienced by many who are beginners in the spiritual life, the night of the spirit is experienced only by those few who are already proficient and have proven themselves in the life of the spirit.

The first night or purgation is bitter and terrible to the life of sense. But the second night is incomparably more dreadful and horrible to the spirit. Since the night of sense is first in order and is experienced first, we shall begin by speaking briefly about it.

Since, as we have pointed out, the behavior of beginners is still very imperfect and infested with self-love and self-will, God desires to lead them onward and raise them from this low stage to a higher degree of love for Him. And when they have practised the life of virtue over a period of time, have persevered in meditation and prayer, have freed themselves from their love for the things of the world and gained some spiritual strength in God, He turns all this light into darkness, shuts the open door and plugs the source of the sweet waters of the spirit which they were permitted to taste as often and as long as their heart desired. He now leaves them in such total darkness that they do not know where to turn with their imagination and their thoughts. They are no longer able to advance another step in meditation, since their internal senses are already deeply submerged in this night and left in such dryness that those spiritual things and devout exercises wherein they formerly found pleasure and delight appear to them bitter and insipid. And all this is for them a new and strange experience, since everything seems to have turned into its opposite.

CHAPTER IX

Three signs indicative of the night of sense.

Since such aridities are sometimes caused by sins and imperfections, by laxity and tepidity, or by some bad humor or bodily indisposition rather than by the trials of the dark night and the purgation of sensual desire, I shall here set down certain signs by which it may be known whether this aridity derives from the purgation of sense or from some of these faults.

The first sign is present when a soul finds no pleasure or consolation in the things of God nor in any created thing. But because this displeasure in heavenly and earthly things might be caused by some bodily indisposition or by melancholy, it is necessary to consider also the second sign and condition.

This second sign is indicated by the fact that ordinarily the memory is [at this stage] concentrated on God with great care and solicitude; and now the soul believes that it is not serving Him, but is sliding backward, because it finds itself without the former sweet joy in the things of God. If this is the case, it is evident that the displeasure and the aridity are not caused by indifference and lukewarmness; for it is the nature of lukewarmness to feel no great inward concern about the things of God. There is then a great difference between aridity and tepidity. And even though— as it sometimes happens—this aridity appears in conjunction with melancholy or some other emotional strain, the purgation of desire is thereby not diminished, since the soul is deprived of all pleasure, and cares about nothing but God. Although—owing to the absence of pleasurable sensations—the sensual part of the soul is weak, inert, and incapable of action, the spirit is agile and strong.

The cause of this aridity lies in the fact that God trans

fers all the goods and powers of sense to the spirit, and as a consequence the senses and the natural strength of the soul remain barren, dry, and empty. The spirit, on the other hand, becomes stronger, more alert, and more solicitous than before. And because of the suddenness with which this change occurs, the spirit does not immediately experience spiritual sweetness and delight, but only aridity and discontent. For we are so deeply immersed in our [sensual] appetites that we long for our miseries and at first abhor the incomparable blessings of Heaven.

When this aridity, then, is caused by the purgation of sensual desire, the inwardly received spiritual food makes the spirit strong for resolute action. And this inner nourishment is the beginning of a contemplation that is dark and arid to the senses, dark and mysterious even to the person who experiences it. And in this state God is leading the soul in such a way and on such a strange path that, if it desires to work with its own powers, it hinders rather than aids the work which God is doing in it. For in this state of contemplation it is God Who is working in the soul: He binds its interior faculties and allows it not to cling to the understanding, nor to rejoice in the will, nor to employ the memory in discursive reasoning. And anything the soul can do in this state by its own power only disturbs its inward peace and the work which God is doing spiritually by means of that aridity of sense.

The third sign whereby this purgation of sense may be recognized is that the soul can no longer meditate or reflect as before and, despite all its efforts, can no longer make use of the internal sense of the imagination. For in this state God no longer communicates Himself to the soul by means of sense and discursive reasoning, but He now begins to communicate Himself by means of the pure spirit or by an act of simple contemplation, for which neither the internal nor the external senses of man have any capacity.

CHAPTER X

*The soul must remain in this dark night in peace and
quiet, but overt to God in prayer.*

As long as the aridity of this night of sense lasts, spiritual
persons suffer great tribulations, not only on account of the
aridity which they experience but also because of their fear
that they may have lost their way. They imagine that they
have lost all spiritual blessings and that God has abandoned
them. Then they unduly exert and exhaust themselves in
the endeavor to find a certain amount of pleasure by con-
centrating their faculties on some object of meditation, in
the mistaken belief that unless they do this they are guilty
of idleness. And while they are thus trying to put their own
mind to work, they lose the spirit of tranquillity and peace.

Now if these souls at such a time find no one who understands them, they go backward: they either abandon the
right path or they lose all courage. And yet all the efforts
they are making to advance further on the road of meditation and discursive reasoning merely weary and overtax
their nature. For all this has become quite unnecessary, since
God is now leading them by another road, which is that of
contemplation and which is wholly different from the first.
Whereas the former was the road of *meditation* and reasoning, the latter leaves no room for either imagination or
rational discourse. And those who find themselves in this
condition should console themselves and persevere in patience; they should not be troubled, but should place their
trust in God, Who does not abandon those who seek Him
with a simple and pure heart. Though it may seem to them
that they are doing nothing and are wasting their time, they
must allow their soul to remain in peace and quiet. They
are doing enough if they have patience and persevere in
prayer. For when the soul places no obstacle in the way of

that infused contemplation which God is bestowing upon it, He refreshes it with greater abundance of peace and causes it to be enkindled and to burn with the spirit of love which this dark and mysterious contemplation communicates to the soul. For contemplation is nothing but a secret, peaceful, and loving infusion from God. And this the soul indicates in the next line of the stanza when it sings:

"My longing heart aglow with love."

CHAPTER XI

Explanation of the last three lines of the stanza, with reference to the passive night of sense.

This flame of love is not as a rule felt in the beginning, because, owing to the impurity of human nature, this love has not yet taken hold of the soul, or because the soul has not yet understood its own novel condition and has therefore not allowed this flame to burn calmly. Sometimes, however, the soul begins to experience a sudden awakening of an intense yearning for God; and the more the soul progresses, the more strongly it finds itself seized and inflamed by love for God, without knowing or understanding how and whence this love and affection have come to it. The soul feels itself wounded by love, and it does not know how this happened. And because at times this flame of love in the spirit burns brighter and brighter, the yearnings for God become so intense in the soul that the very bones seem to be dried up by this thirst, and the bodily nature, its warmth and its vital strength, seem to be fading away and die.

The third line: "Oh, blessed lot."

God leads the soul into this night of sense in order to purge the life of sense, to subdue it, to conform the sense to the spirit and eventually to unite it with the spirit. In a similar manner God afterwards leads the soul into the night of the spirit, in order to purify the spirit and unite it with Him. And herein the soul gains so many blessings that it calls it a "blessed lot" to have escaped by means of this night from the snares and bonds of its lower sensual self. These blessings are all implied in the fourth line of the stanza: *"I went forth unseen."*

The fourth line: "I went forth unseen."

This "going forth" refers to the former subjection of the soul to its sensual part. For [in its former condition] the soul stumbled at every step into numerous imperfections and follies, as we noted above when we treated of the seven capital sins. From all these defects the soul is now freed. And it is indeed a "blessed lot" or a great good fortune when, by means of this night, the soul goes forth from all created things and journeys toward eternal things, because there are very few who patiently persevere until they enter by this small gate onto the narrow road which, as Our Saviour says, leads to life (cf. Matt. 7:14). The small gate is this night of sense, in which the soul deprives and empties itself of all things. It now is grounded in and supported by faith, so that afterwards it may travel by the narrow path of the second night—the night of the spirit.

CHAPTER XII

The benefits deriving from this night: knowledge of self and of God; humility; love of neighbor.

The first and principal benefit which the soul derives from this arid and dark night of contemplation is the knowledge of its own self and its own misery. For these aridities and the emptiness of the faculties make the soul recognize its own lowliness, which it was unable to see when it was happy and prosperous. Now, however, it has no longer any self-esteem or self-satisfaction; for it realizes that of itself it neither does nor is capable of doing anything. And this absence of self-satisfaction, together with the sorrow the soul feels at not serving God, is valued by God much more highly than all its former good works and sweet feelings. From this self-knowledge, however, derive a number of other benefits as from their source and origin.

First of all, the soul becomes much more reverent and modest in its communion with God. This is well exemplified by Job, whom God, when He wanted to speak to him, did not prepare by giving him those delights and glories which, according to his own testimony, he had formerly enjoyed, but by leaving him naked upon a dung-hill, abandoned and even persecuted by his friends, and filled with bitterness and anguish. And only then the Most High God, "Who lifts up the poor man from the dung-hill," deigned to come down and speak with Job face to face; and only now did He reveal to him the hidden treasures of His wisdom, as He had never done in the days of Job's prosperity.

In this dark night the word of the prophet is fulfilled: "Thy light shall shine in the darkness" (Is. 58:10). God here illumines the soul by giving it knowledge not only of its own lowliness and misery but also of the greatness of His Divine Majesty. For, after the desires, pleasures, and attachments of sense have been quenched, the mind remains free for the understanding of the Truth. And thus we see clearly that from this arid night comes first of all self-knowledge, and this in turn is the foundation from which arises the knowledge of God. This is why St. Augustine said to God: "Let me know myself, oh Lord, and I shall know Thee" (*Soliloq.,* chap. 2). For, as the philosophers say, one extreme can be known best by another. This dark night, then, is the means to the knowledge of oneself and of God, even though it does not lead to that plenitude and abundance of knowledge which derive from the night of the spirit; for this knowledge is only the beginning of the other kind.

In the aridity and emptiness of this night of the desire

[of sense] the soul also grows in spiritual humility, the virtue which is the direct opposite of spiritual pride, the first capital sin. And this humility of spirit engenders the love of our neighbor.

CHAPTER XIII

Further benefits: spiritual sobriety; practice of all virtues; the twelve fruits of the Holy Spirit.

As far as the imperfections caused by spiritual avarice are concerned, this arid and dark night produces a complete transformation of the soul in this respect also. Those whom God leads into this night do everything that is demanded of them purely for God's sake, even though they find no satisfaction whatever in doing it.

As regards spiritual impurity, it is evident that by this aridity and by the absence of sweetness in spiritual experiences the soul is freed from all the previously mentioned imperfections; for, as we have pointed out, these imperfections proceed as a rule from the pleasure which overflows from the spirit into the sensual appetite.

To understand the innumerable benefits which the soul gains in this night by its victory over the sin of spiritual gluttony, it suffices to say that God now restrains the soul's inordinate desires, so that it can no longer feed on any sweetness and pleasure of sense. And this He continues to do until the soul is subdued and completely transformed with respect to all such desires. The soul dries up, as it were, because it can no longer indulge its likings. And from this wonderful spiritual sobriety follow further great benefits; for, when the desires are subjugated and silenced, the soul lives in spiritual tranquillity and in peace.

Another and very great benefit is the steadfast practice of all the virtues. For example, the soul practises patience and perseverance when, in the midst of this aridity and inward emptiness, it patiently continues in its spiritual exercises, without receiving any consolation or refreshment. It practises the love of God, since it is now no longer motivated by the pleasure of attraction and the experience of sweetness, but only by God. And it practises the virtue of fortitude; for in all the difficulties and vexations which it finds in its work, it draws strength from weakness and thus becomes strong. In short, in these aridities the soul learns to practise all the virtues—the theological as well as the cardinal and moral.

And as regards the imperfections which derive from the other three spiritual sins—anger, envy, and spiritual sloth—the soul is purged of them likewise in this aridity of desire, and it acquires the virtues opposed to them. Softened and humbled by these aridities and hardships as well as by other temptations and trials with which God tests the soul during this night, it attains to peace with God, with itself, and with its neighbor. It is no longer angry with itself because of its own faults, nor with its neighbor because of his faults; and it no longer gives voice to irreverent complaints because God does not make it perfect in a single day. And as to spiritual envy, the soul knows now only love for all fellow-souls. Seeing its own misery, it grieves not when others are preferred to it, and its envy (if it has any) has now become a virtue, since it consists in the desire to emulate others, which is indeed a sign of great virtue.

Finally, as the soul is now purged from all affections and desires of sense, it gains freedom of spirit and concomitantly the twelve fruits of the Holy Ghost. It is delivered at last from the hands of its three enemies—the devil, the world, and the flesh; for, once it has died to the pleasure and delight of sense with respect to all things, it has disarmed the devil, the world, and sensuality: they have no longer the strength to wage war against the spirit.

In souls which experience this arid night, the anxious care to serve God increases steadily. And this is very pleasing to God, for, as David says, a contrite spirit is a sacrifice to God (cf. Ps. 50:19). The soul now knows that in this arid purgation it has gained so many and precious blessings that it cries out exultantly:

> "Oh, blessed lot!
> I went forth unseen."

The soul means to say: In darkness, unseen, I escaped and fled from the bonds and the servitude of the desires and affections of sense; and the three enemies were unable to hinder my escape.

When, therefore, the four passions of the soul—joy, grief, hope, and fear—have been calmed by continuous self-denial; when the natural desires have been put to sleep by the aridity of the sensual part, and when the harmonious inter-action of the senses and the internal faculties has caused a suspension and cessation of the discursive and reflective operations of the soul, then the three enemies can no longer obstruct the freedom of the spirit, and the soul can say:

> "My house was at last in deepest rest."

CHAPTER XIV

*The last line of the first stanza: "My house was at rest":
the way of illumination.*

When this house of sensuality was at last at rest—that is, when the senses were mortified by means of this blessed night, the passions silenced, the desires appeased and put to sleep—the soul went forth to begin its journey on the road of the spirit. This is the way of those who have progressed and become proficient in the spiritual life, and it is also known as *the way of illumination* or *infused contemplation*. On this road it is God Himself Who spiritually nourishes and refreshes, without the active help of the soul. This, then, is *the passive night and purgation of sense.* And in those who afterwards are to enter into the second and much more severe night of the spirit, in order to attain to the supernatural union of love with God, this first night is usually accompanied by severe trials and sensual temptations. Some are visited by an angel of Satan—the spirit of impurity—who torments their senses with violent and abominable temptations, so that at times their affliction is worse than death.

At other times there is added to the trials of this night the spirit of blasphemy, which fills all their thoughts and ideas with all kinds of intolerable blasphemies. Again, at other times, they are attacked by another abominable spirit, known as the spirit of dizziness (*Spiritus vertiginis,* cf. Is. 19:14), not in order to cause them to fall, but in order to try and test them. This spirit darkens their senses and fills their minds with a thousand scruples and with such confusion and perplexity that they remain restless and dissatisfied and are unable to submit their judgment to any counsel or advice. And this is one of the most severe and horrible temptations of this night of sense, very closely akin to what happens in the night of the spirit.

With these tempests and trials God usually visits and tests those whom He afterwards leads into the night of the spirit. Thus chastened and buffeted, they are to exercise and harden their senses and faculties to prepare them for the union with wisdom which will be theirs in the night of the spirit. For, unless the soul be exercised and tested by trials and temptations, its senses cannot grow mature for the union with wisdom. This is why it is said in Ecclesiasticus: "He who has not been tempted, what does he know? And without experience, a man knows little" (34:9-10).

Those who have a greater capacity and strength for suffering, God purges quicker and more thoroughly. Those, on the other hand, who are weaker, He tests with only mild temptations and with great forbearance, but He leaves them in this night for a longer period of time and often refreshes their senses so that they may not turn backward. And for this reason they attain to perfect purity in this life only after a long time, and some of them not at all. From other souls, which are still weaker, God at times withholds and hides His presence, in order to test their love; for otherwise they would never learn to reach God.

But now the time has come to begin our discourse of the second night.

BOOK TWO

The Night of the Spirit

CHAPTER I

The time of the beginning of this night; its general effects.

The soul which God wants to lead onward is not brought into the night of the spirit immediately after it has emerged from the aridities and trials of the night of sense. Years may pass, during which the soul, after having left the state of beginners, is exercising itself in the more advanced stages of the spiritual life. Such a soul feels as if it had escaped from a narrow prison cell, and it is now able to devote itself to the things of God with much greater freedom and satisfaction. Its imagination and its faculties are no longer bound by meditation and by definite rules of the spiritual life, since it now enjoys in its spirit a very serene and loving contemplation without the labor of meditation. But the most important thing—the purgation of the spirit—is still lacking, and without this, owing to the intimate interconnection between sense and spirit in man, the purification of the soul cannot be complete and perfect. And for this reason the soul finds itself rarely without certain afflictions, aridities, darknesses, and anxieties, whicn are sometimes much more intense than those it experienced in the past; for these former experiences were like omens and messengers of the coming night of the spirit, but they did not last as long as will the night which is to come. For, after the soul has been in this [first] night and its tempests for some time, the former serenity of mind returns.

The sweetness and inward delight which those advanced

183

in the spiritual life experience in their spirits are communicated to them much more abundantly than was formerly the case, and these delights overflow into the sensual
part of their nature much more perceptibly than prior to
this purgation of sense. For, inasmuch as the senses are now
more purified, they have acquired a greater capacity for
tasting the delights of the spirit. But owing to the fact that
the sensual part of the soul is still too weak and thus incapable of receiving into itself the full power of the spirit,
these advanced souls—because of the interaction and communication between spirit and sense—suffer as a rule from
many physical weaknesses or digestive disturbances, and in
consequence also from spiritual fatigue. For, as the Wise
Man says: "The soul is weighed down by a corruptible body"
(Wisd. 9:15). This is why these communications cannot be
as strong, intense, and spiritual as is required for supernatural union with God. And this weakness and corruption
of the sensual part of human nature accounts also for the
raptures, ecstasies, and convulsions, which as a rule occur
when these communications are not purely spiritual, that is,
when they are not given to the spirit alone, as happens in
the case of the perfect, who are purified by the night of
the spirit and in whom all raptures and torments of the
body have come to an end, since they are enjoying the
freedom of the spirit, and their senses are no longer either
clouded or transported.

CHAPTER II

*Imperfections of those advanced in the spiritual life:
dullness of mind, inaptitude, distraction, vanity, etc.*

Those advanced in the spiritual life have *two kinds of imperfections:* the one kind is long lasting or *habitual,* the other
temporary or actual. The habitual imperfections are inclina-

tions which have, as it were, struck deep roots in the spirit, so that the purgation of sense was unable to reach them.

These souls suffer from *hebetudo mentis* [dullness of spirit] and from that natural inaptitude which every human being contracts through original sin. In addition, they suffer from distraction of the spirit and from a lack of true inwardness. These imperfections must be healed by the afflictions and sufferings of the dark night of the spirit. And all who have not passed beyond this state of progressives are afflicted with these habitual imperfections. They are incompatible, on the other hand, with the perfect state of union with God.

As far as the *temporary or actual imperfections* are concerned, not all are subject to them in the same manner and degree. Some fall into greater difficulties and dangers than others. And many persons in this state are induced by the devil to believe in vain visions and false prophecies. He awakens in them the delusion and presumption that God and the saints were speaking with them, whereas actually they were merely listening to the suggestions of their own fancy. And, moved by vanity and arrogance, they often allow themselves to be seen in acts which have the external appearance of holiness, such as raptures and similar phenomena. They then become overbearing in their attitude toward God, and they lose holy fear, the key and the custodian of all virtues. And they fall into these miseries because in the early stages of their spiritual progress they had given themselves over to spiritual feelings and vain imaginings with too much self-assurance.

To attain, then, to union with God, the soul must enter into the second [or passive] night of the spirit, wherein it must totally denude both sense and spirit of all apprehensions and all sensory feelings, and must walk in darkness and pure faith, which is the proper and adequate means of union with God.

CHAPTER III

The purgation effected by passive and dark contemplation.

The purgation of sense will become fully effective only when the purgation of the spirit begins in earnest. The night of sense, therefore, should be called a transformation and a restraining of desire rather than a genuine purgation. The reason is that all the imperfections and disorders of the sensual part of human nature have their root and the source of their strength in the spirit, where all good and bad habits originate. And thus, until these are purged, the rebellions and disorders of sense cannot be completely overcome. In the night which is to follow, therefore, both parts of the soul are purged together. This is a necessary prerequisite for such a thoroughgoing and rigorous purgation; for, if the weakness of the lower part were not first corrected, the nature of the soul would have neither the fortitude nor the capacity to bear the trials of that dark night.

Since these advanced souls, then, are not yet in possession of the purified and resplendent gold of the spirit, their dealings and communications with God are still at a very low stage. They still think of God as children, they speak of Him as children, and their knowledge and feelings concerning Him are those of children (cf. St. Paul, 1 Cor. 13:11). This shows that they have not yet reached perfection, that is, the union of the soul with God. But when they will have attained to that state of union, then they will act as grown men, performing great works in the spirit, and their works and faculties will then be more Divine than human. Then God will denude their faculties, affections, and feelings—both spiritual and sensual, external and internal—leaving the understanding in darkness, the will in dryness, and the memory in emptiness; filling the affections of the soul with deepest sadness, bitterness, and tribulation, and depriving the soul of all the former experience and enjoyment of spiritual goods. For this privation is one of the pre-conditions which must be fulfilled in the spirit if it is to become capable of receiving and being united with the spiritual form of the spirit, which is the union of love.

All this the Lord works in the soul by means of a pure and dark contemplation, as is intimated by the soul in the first stanza. Although the meaning of this stanza has already been explained with reference to the first night of sense, these lines have a more direct bearing on the experiences of the soul during the second night of the spirit, since this latter constitutes the most important part of the purification of the soul. And for this reason we shall set it down and explain it here again.

CHAPTER IV

Second explanation of the first stanza. The second night of the spirit: the union of love.

> In a dark night,
> My longing heart aglow with love,
> —Oh, blessed lot!—
> I went forth unseen
> From my house that was at last at rest.

We shall now interpret this stanza with reference to the purgation, contemplation, denudation, or perfect poverty of the spirit. Understanding the words, then, in this sense, the soul says: In poverty, unprotected and unsupported by any apprehensions, that is, in the darkness of my understanding, in the constraint of my will, and in the affliction and anguish of my memory, I gave myself over to that darkness of pure faith, which is indeed a dark night for all the natural faculties. While my will was filled wholly with sorrows, with afflictions, and with yearnings for the love of God, I went forth from myself, that is, from my low manner of understanding, from my half-hearted way of loving, and from my poor and limited manner of experiencing the presence of God—I went forth, without being hindered by either sensuality or by the enemy. This was a great happiness and a blessed lot for me; for, no sooner had I subdued and silenced the faculties, the passions, the desires, and the affections of my soul, than I went forth from my own poor human way and work and proceeded to the way and order of God. That is to say, my understanding went forth from itself and was transformed from a human into a Divine understanding. It was united with God by means of this purgation, so that now it no longer operates through its own natural light and strength, but through the Divine Wisdom with which it has become united. And my will went forth from itself and became a Divine will: being united with Divine love, it no longer loves with its limited natural strength, but by virtue of the strength and purity of the Holy Spirit. And in a similar manner my memory has been transformed and is now engaged in the apprehension of the glories of eternal life. And finally, by means of this night and purgation of the old man, all the energies and affections of the soul are wholly transformed into Divine qualities and have become sources of Divine joys.

CHAPTER V

"In a dark night": this dark infused contemplation entails much suffering.

This dark night is an inflowing of God into the soul, which purges it from its ignorance and its habitual—natural and spiritual—imperfections. The theologians call it *infused contemplation* and treat of it in *mystical theology*. In this state God mysteriously teaches the soul the perfection of love, without its doing anything and without its understanding the nature of this infused contemplation. For what produces such striking effects in the soul is the loving wisdom of God, which by its purifying and illuminating action prepares the soul for the union of love with God. And this loving wisdom is the same which also purifies and illumines the blessed spirits.

But now the question arises: Why does the soul call this Divine light a dark night? The answer is that for two reasons this Divine wisdom is for the soul not only night and darkness, but also affliction and torment. The first reason is the sublime grandeur of Divine Wisdom, which transcends the capacity of the soul and is therefore darkness to it. The second reason is the lowliness and impurity of the soul, and in this respect Divine Wisdom is for the soul painful, bitter, and dark.

In order to prove the first point, we must refer to a doctrine of the Philosopher [i.e., Aristotle], which says that, the clearer and more manifest Divine things are in themselves, the darker and more hidden they are to the soul; just as, the brighter the light is, the more it blinds and darkens the eye of the night-owl. When, therefore, this Divine light of contemplation invades a soul which is not yet wholly illumined, it causes spiritual darkness in it; for it not only transcends the soul's natural intellectual capacity, but it also drowns out and darkens the act of intellection. This is why Dionysius [the Areopagite] and other mystical theologians call this infused contemplation a ray of darkness for the soul that is not yet wholly purified and illumined.

And [with respect to the second point] it is clear that this dark contemplation is in its early stages very painful to the soul; for, as this Divine infused contemplation comprises in itself a plentitude of the highest perfections, and since the soul which receives them is not yet wholly purified and thus still engulfed in a sea of miseries, it follows that —because two contraries cannot coexist in one subject— the soul must of necessity endure much pain and suffering.

Thus, when this pure light invades the soul, in order to expel its impurity, the soul feels its own impurity so intensely that it believes God to be its enemy and comes to think of itself as an enemy of God. This causes it so much grief and sadness that it feels actually rejected and forsaken by God. And what gives it the greatest pain is the fear that it will never be worthy of God and that therefore all its blessings are lost for ever. For this Divine and dark light now reveals to the soul's sight all its faults and miseries, so that it may see clearly how by its own powers it can never have anything else.

The second kind of torment which the soul suffers is caused by its natural, moral, and spiritual weakness; for, when this Divine contemplation takes hold of the soul with some degree of violence, in order to strengthen it and make it obedient, it suffers so much pain in its weakness that it almost faints. Both sense and spirit suffer such pain and agony as if they were weighed down by some immense load, so that even death would appear as a release and relief. And it is indeed very strange and very sad that the soul is so weak and impure that the light and gentle hand of God appears to it as such a prodigious weight and such a hostile force, since this hand does not really weigh the soul down, but only touches it mercifully, in order to bestow favors and graces upon it.

CHAPTER VI

Other sufferings of the dark night: spiritual death; dereliction; forlornness.

The third kind of sufferings and torments which the soul has to endure in this state is caused by the fact that two other extremes—the Divine and the human—meet in this night. The Divine extreme is this purgative contemplation itself, while the human extreme is the individual soul. The

Divine invades the soul in order to renew it and super-naturalize it by stripping it of the habitual affections and attachments of the old man. God crushes and consumes the spiritual substance of the soul and envelops it in such deep and black darkness that the soul believes itself to be perishing in a dreadful spiritual death.

These sufferings and torments, although in truth they defy all description, are indicated by David, when he exclaims: "All about me sounded the lamentations of death; the torments of hell surrounded me; I cried to the Lord in my tribulation" (Ps. 17:5-7). But what the sorrowing soul feels most painfully in this condition is the dreadful thought that God has abandoned it and has flung it into utter darkness. For indeed, when this purgative contemplation takes hold of the soul, it feels most vividly the shadows and laments of death and the torments of hell, which consist in the conviction that God in His anger has chastised and forsaken it for ever, because it has shown itself unworthy of Him.

The fourth kind of pain is caused in the soul by another perfection of this dark contemplation, namely, its majesty and sublimity. And this leads the soul to an acute awareness of the other extreme, namely, its own profound poverty and great misery. It feels within itself a profound emptiness and deprivation of three kinds of goods—temporal, natural, and spiritual; and it finds itself in the midst of the evils that are the opposites of these goods, namely, the miseries of its imperfection, the aridity and emptiness of the faculties of apprehension, and the dereliction and forlornness of the spirit in darkness. For the sensual part of the soul must be purified by aridity, the faculties by their being emptied of all apprehensions, and the spirit by massive darkness. Moreover, God is purifying the soul by annihilating or consuming in it all the affections and habitual imperfections which it has contracted during its whole life, even as fire consumes the rust and the mouldiness of metal. Since, however, these imperfections are deeply rooted in the substance of the soul, severe bodily and internal torments are usually added to the aforementioned natural and spiritual poverty and emptiness. And because the soul, according to the saying of the Wise Man, is purified in this furnace like gold in the crucible (cf. Wisd. 3:6), it is so keenly aware in its substance of its being wholly consumed in this fire that, realizing its extreme poverty, it almost expires. Here God greatly humbles the soul, in order that afterwards He may exalt it all the more.

Such souls descend in truth into the netherworld [of purgatory], for they are purged here on earth in the same manner as there, since this purgation is of the kind they would have to suffer in purgatory. And thus the soul which suffers here in this manner either does not enter that place [of purgatory] at all, or is detained there only a very short time; for one hour of this purgation here benefits the soul more than do many hours there.

CHAPTER VII

Afflictions and trials of the will.

The afflictions and trials of the will, too, are exceedingly great in this state, especially since as a rule souls which enter into this night have previously found many sweetnesses in God and have rendered Him many services. And so numerous and grievous are these sufferings, and so many passages of Holy Scripture could be cited in this regard, that time and strength would fail us if we wanted to mention them all.

The soul is as helpless in this state as a prisoner who lies, bound hand and foot, in a dark dungeon, and can neither move, nor see, nor receive any message of consolation from earth or from Heaven. And this suffering lasts until the soul has become humble, gentle, and pure in spirit, and so wise, simple, and poor that it can become one with the Spirit of God.

But if this purgation is to be really effective, it will have to last for several years, however severe it may be. But during this time there are intervals of relief when, by the dispensation of God, this dark contemplation works upon the soul not in the manner of purgation but rather in an illuminative and loving manner. Then the soul feels like one who has been liberated from his dungeon and freed from his chains, and it enjoys the great blessings of freedom, peace, and loving friendship with God. All this is to the soul a sign of health and a foretaste of the abundance which it anticipates in its hope.

As long, however, as this spiritual purification is not complete, these sweet communications are rarely given to the soul in such abundance as to keep from its sight the remaining root [of imperfection]: the soul is aware that there is still something wanting within itself and that the work toward its perfection must continue. Thus it cannot fully enjoy that refreshment, for it feels that there is still an enemy within, an enemy who, though temporarily subdued and asleep, must still be feared, since he may come to life again and continue his evil work. And this is actually so; for, precisely when the soul feels most secure, this enemy seeks to assail it again and tries to drag it down into a depth of suffering, severer, darker, and more excruciating than before. And once again the soul comes to believe that it has for ever been deprived of all its blessings. And thus, although the soul in this purgation is quite aware that it has a great love for God, and is willing to give a thousand lives for Him, this is no consolation to it, but rather makes it suffer all the more. For the soul now loves God so much that it no longer cares and is anxious about anything else; and when it still sees itself in such misery, it cannot believe that God loves it, but is convinced that there is every reason why not only He but all creatures should for ever abhor it.

CHAPTER VIII

Other torments: inability to pray, absent-mindedness, weakness of memory, etc.

There is yet another thing which grieves and afflicts the soul greatly in this state. For, as this dark night has arrested the soul's faculties and affections in such a high degree, it is no longer able to raise its heart and mind to God as it did before, nor is it able to pray. And if it sometimes does pray, it remains so dry and devoid of feeling that it is convinced that God neither hears its prayer nor pays any attention to it. But, as a matter of fact, this is not the proper time for the soul to speak to God in prayer; it should rather, as Jeremiah says, "kiss the dust with its mouth" (Lam. 3:29), so that perchance some ray of hope may enlighten it, and it may be able to endure this purgation with patience. For it is God Who is working here in the soul, and this is why the soul can do nothing. And for the same reason it can neither pray nor attentively assist at the Divine services, and much less can it attend to other things and temporal affairs. It even suffers at times from such absent-mindedness and such forgetfulness and weakness of the memory that many hours pass by without its knowing what it has been doing or thinking, or what it is doing now or is going to do next. This absent-mindedness and forgetfulness, however, are caused by the soul's being completely absorbed in this contemplation. And thus, the simpler and purer this Divine light enters the soul, the more it darkens, empties, and annihilates the soul with respect to particular apprehensions and affections.

Now it sounds quite incredible when we say that the brighter and purer this supernatural and Divine light is, the more it darkens the soul, and that the less bright and pure it is, the less dark it appears to the soul. But this [seeming paradox] is easily understood if we remember what has been proved above by the saying of the Philosopher—namely, that the brighter and the more manifest supernatural things are in themselves, the darker they are to our understanding.

This Divine ray of contemplation, then, strikes the soul with its Divine light and thus darkens it and deprives it of all natural apprehensions and affections which it previously had perceived and felt by means of the natural light. And thus it leaves the soul not only in darkness, but also empties it with respect to its spiritual and natural faculties and desires. And when the soul is thus empty and in darkness, this ray purifies and illumines it with Divine spiritual light, even though the soul may be unaware as yet of this illumination and may think that it is still in darkness. But when this spiritual light which penetrates the soul strikes upon something, that is, when something presents itself to the spiritual understanding, such as the spiritual insight into the nature of perfection, or a judgment concerning the truth or falsehood of something, then the soul sees and understands with much greater clarity than it did before it entered into this darkness.

Since, then, this spiritual light is so simple, pure, and general and not limited or confined to any particularized natural or supernatural knowledge, it follows that the soul now easily discerns and penetrates with one general comprehensive act of knowledge whatever presents itself to it, whether it be of Heaven or of the earth. This is why St. Paul says of the spiritual man that he searches and penetrates all things, even the depths of God (cf. 1 Cor. 2:10). And it is the mark of the spirit (that has been purged and annihilated with respect to all particular affections and all particularized knowledge) that, remaining in emptiness and darkness, it takes pleasure in no particular thing and understands no particular thing, but is capable of embracing all things in their totality. The spiritual man thus exemplifies what St. Paul meant when he said: "They own nothing, but possess everything" (2 Cor. 6:10).

CHAPTER IX

*This night darkens the spirit, but only in order to
illuminate it. The mystical union.*

This blissful night darkens the spirit, but only in order to
illuminate it afterwards with respect to all things; it humbles
the spirit and makes it miserable, but only in order to raise
it up and exalt it; it impoverishes the spirit and deprives it
of every natural possession and affection, but only to enable
it to rise, divinely, in unfettered spiritual freedom, to a perfect fruition of all things in Heaven and on earth. And,
owing to its purity, the spirit tastes the sweetness of all
things in a preeminently sublime manner.

We know that the children of Israel could not relish, in
the desert, the sweetness of the manna—the bread of angels
—solely because they had retained a single affectionate remembrance of the fleshpots and meals which they had tasted
in Egypt. Similarly, the spirit cannot attain to the delights
of the supernatural as long as it remains attached to any
actual or habitual desire or to any particular object or apprehension of the understanding.

The light which is here imparted to the soul is truly a
most sublime Divine light, which transcends every natural
light, and which cannot be grasped by the understanding in
a natural manner. If, then, the understanding is to be united
with this light and is to become Divine in the state of perfection, it must first be purged and annihilated with respect
to its natural light and led into darkness by means of this
dark contemplation. When this has been done, the Divine
light and illumination will take the place of the natural mode
and manner of the soul's understanding.

Moreover, in order to attain to the union to which this
dark night is leading it, the soul must be filled with a certain
glorious splendor, to become disposed for its communion

with God. Included herein are innumerable blessings and delights which far exceed all the abundance which the soul can naturally possess. For, as Isaiah says: "No eye has seen, and no ear has heard, nor has it ever entered into a human heart, what God has prepared for those who love Him" (Is. 64:4). And this is the reason why the soul must first become empty and poor in spirit and purged from all natural support, so that, in total poverty of spirit and liberated from the old man, it may be able to live that new and blessed life which is attained by means of this night, and which is the state of union with God.

In this manner, then, this night is gradually drawing the spirit away from its ordinary and lowly experience of things, in order to fill it with supernatural insight. And at times everything appears so strange and unaccustomed to the soul that it feels as enchanted or as in a trance; and it goes about marvelling at the things it sees and hears, although they are no different from those to which it was accustomed before. The reason of this is that the soul is now becoming estranged from the ordinary ways of thinking and knowing, so that, in dying to these, it may be informed with a knowledge that belongs more to the next life than to this.

Furthermore, by means of this night of contemplation the soul is being prepared for an inward tranquillity and peace, which are so profound and so blissful that, according to Holy Scripture, they surpass all understanding (cf. Phil. 4:7). And for this reason the soul must now abandon all its former peace which, since it was still full of imperfections, was really no peace in the true sense. The soul must therefore first of all be purged of that former "peace": it must be stirred up and must relinquish this false peace, so that it may exclaim with Jeremiah: "Cast out and far away is the peace of my soul" (Lam. 3:17). And this experience produces in the soul such deep sighing and pain that it sometimes groans and cries in spiritual agony, while at other times it may find relief in streams of tears. And just as the waters sometimes are rushing on with such vehemence that they flood and inundate everything, so this roaring and this affliction of the soul become occasionally so overwhelming that they inundate and engulf the soul completely, filling all its inner affections and faculties with spiritual pain and anguish.

These, then, are some of the effects which this night causes in the soul by veiling and clouding all hope for the light of day. And this strife is being fought in the deep interiority of the soul because the peace, too, for which the soul hopes will be a very deep interior peace. And the spiritual pain is so inward and so all-pervasive because the love which the soul will possess will be equally intimate and pure.

CHAPTER X

The purgation of the soul is compared with the burning of wood.

This purgative and loving knowledge or Divine light acts upon the soul which is being purified and prepared for perfect union with God in the same way as fire acts upon a piece of wood that is being transformed into fire; for as soon as material fire is applied to wood it first of all begins to dry it, by driving out the moisture. Then the fire begins to blacken the wood and causes it to look dark and ugly, and gradually drives out all the elements which are contrary to the nature of fire. Finally, the fire begins to heat and kindle the wood and thus eventually transforms it into itself, imparting to it the beauty of fire. And after that the wood has no longer any activity or passivity of its own, for it now has received into itself all the properties and activities of fire.

And in the same way we must understand and judge the nature of this Divine fire of contemplation, which, before it transforms the soul and unites it to itself, purges it of all the elements which are contrary to this Divine fire. It drives out the soul's ugliness, but, in doing so, it first makes the soul black and dark, so that it appears worse than before. For this Divine purgation consumes in the soul all those evil and malicious inclinations which it had never clearly recognized before because they are so deeply rooted and ingrained in the soul. But now that these evil inclinations are about to be driven out and annihilated, they rise before the soul's eye and are seen in the dark light of contemplation.

Incidentally, we can derive from this comparison some knowledge of the nature of the suffering of souls in purgatory. For the fire would have no power over them if they had no imperfections and faults which make them capable of suffering. For these faults furnish the fuel for that fire, and when this fuel is consumed, there is nothing left that can burn.

CHAPTER XI

Explanation of the second line: "My longing heart aglow with love." The fruit of these afflictions is a vehement passion of Divine love.

In this line the soul describes this fire of love which, as we have said, begins to take hold upon the soul in this painful night of contemplation. This "being aglow" of the soul, although in some respects it resembles the enkindling which we described above as coming to pass in the sensual part of the soul, in other respects it is as different from it as the soul from the body or the spiritual part from the sensual. For in the midst of these dark afflictions the soul here feels itself wounded in the spirit by a flame of love, and it has a certain presentiment or foretaste of God, without, however, understanding any particular thing, since, as we have mentioned, the understanding is in darkness. And this spiritual flame produces a passionate love, which, inasmuch as it is an infused love, manifests itself passively rather than actively, in suffering rather than in doing. And this love has already in it something of the union with God and to some extent shares in the properties of that union, so that all the soul has to do here is to give its consent to the actions of God.

In this dark purgation, then, God has so weaned and recollected all the inclinations of the soul that they can no longer find pleasure in anything. All this He does to detach the soul from all things and to draw it to Himself. And in this purgative state the soul must love with the strength of all its spiritual and sensory powers and desires, which it could not do if it were to disperse its strength in the enjoyment of anything else.

When the soul then says in this line: "My longing heart aglow with love," it is because in all the things and thoughts with which it preoccupies itself, and in all affairs and situations in which it finds itself involved, it loves and longs and suffers in ever so many ways; and finds no rest and contentment in anything, because everything has become too narrow. And the soul's yearning and grief in this glowing love are all the greater because they are fed in two ways: first, by the spiritual darkness in which the soul finds itself, which afflicts it with doubts and anxieties; second, by the love of God, which inflames and incites the soul with this wound of love and completely overawes it. But in the midst of this dark and loving affliction the soul feels within itself the strength of a guiding force which so envigorates it that, when the burden of this oppressive darkness is removed, it often feels itself abandoned, empty, and weak. The reason of this is that this strength was granted and communicated to the soul passively (that is, without any activity of its own) by the dark and all-pervasive fire of love; consequently, when that fire ceases to burn, the darkness, the power, and the heat of love in the soul likewise disappear.

CHAPTER XII

This dreadful night resembles purgatory. In this night Divine Wisdom illumines men on earth with the same light that purges and illumines the angels. Infused love and infused knowledge.

From what has been said we can see how this dark night of the fire of love not only purges the soul in darkness but also enkindles it in darkness. We can likewise see that, just as the spirits are purged in the next life with dark material fire, so in this life they are purged and cleansed with the dark and spiritual fire of love. The only difference is that in the next life they are cleansed with fire, while here on earth they are purified and illumined with love. For the purity of heart is nothing but the [infused] love and grace of God. The pure of heart—that is, those "enkindled with love"—Our Saviour calls "blessed"; for blessedness is granted only if one pays the price of love.

We can infer furthermore that the Wisdom of God which purifies and illumines these souls is the very same wisdom which purges the angels of their ignorance. For this wisdom emanates from God and flows down from the highest hierarchies to the lowest, and from them to men. All the works, therefore, which are done by the angels, and all the inspirations which they communicate are in a true and real sense primarily the work of God and only secondarily their own.

It follows, then, that the nearer the higher and lower spirits are to God, the more thoroughly are they purged and illumined; and that the lowest of them will receive the illumination in a weaker manner, because they are farther removed from God. It follows furthermore that man—who is the lowest of all those spirits to whom this love-inspiring contemplation flows down from God—will, if God deigns to give it to him, receive it of necessity in a much more limited manner and with much pain, in accordance with the more limited capacity of human nature.

As time goes on and this fire of love begins to infuse its heat, the soul as a rule becomes conscious of this inwardly burning flame of love. But, as now the understanding is being more and more purified by means of this darkness, it sometimes happens that this mystical and loving Wisdom of God, in addition to enkindling the will, also touches and illumines the understanding, so that it now seems to the soul that it is receiving living fire with living understanding. And this flame of love in these two faculties of the soul—the understanding and the will—is a great treasure and delight to the soul; for it is a sign that the soul has already come in touch with the Godhead and that it is nearing that state of perfect union for which it hopes.

From what we have said here it may be inferred that in the communication of these spiritual blessings, which are infused by God into the soul passively [that is, without any activity on the part of the soul], it may easily happen that the will is filled with love, while the understanding remains in unknowing; or that the understanding is capable of knowing, while the will is not enkindled with love, just as—to use a comparison—it may happen that one feels the heat of fire without seeing the flame, or that one sees the flame without feeling the heat that issues from it. All these things are worked by the Lord, Who communicates Himself as He wills.

CHAPTER XIII

Other blessings produced by this dark night. Night of sense and night of spirit. The divinization of the soul.

Sometimes the soul is filled with light in the midst of all this darkness, and then truly "the light shines in the darkness"

(John 1:5). This mystical knowledge flows into the understanding, while the will remains in dryness, without actually partaking of this union of love; and meanwhile the sensual part of the soul is in such a delicate and serene quiet and simplicity that no words can be found to describe it; and the presence of God is experienced now in one way, and now in another.

Sometimes, too, as has been said, this flame of love wounds the will [and the understanding] simultaneously and causes love to burn ardently, tenderly, and strongly; for, as we have already stated, these two faculties are at times more perfectly and more sublimely united when the understanding is more thoroughly purified. But before the soul reaches this state, it usually feels the effect of this enkindling in the will, prior to experiencing the influx of knowledge in the understanding.

The burning fervor and thirst of love, which are here induced by the Holy Spirit, are wholly different from the experiences we described when we were writing on the *night of sense.* For, although here too the senses participate in this burning love, since they are sharing in the afflictions of the spirit, yet this thirst of love is felt most intensely and most vitally in the higher part of the soul, that is, in the *spirit.* And the spirit is so keenly aware of what it feels and of the absence of what it desires, that all the affliction of sense—although this latter is incomparably greater than it was in the first night of sense—appears as nothing; for the spirit now recognizes within its own innermost being the lack of a good that is great and sublime beyond all measure.

It is characteristic of all deep and true love that all things seem possible to it. This kind of love is convinced that no one can possibly be engaged or interested in anything save in that which itself seeks and loves. And of this kind are the anxious yearnings of the love of which a soul that has made progress in this spiritual purgation gains an inward experience. In this purgative darkness the soul rises by night and goes forth to seek its God, not unlike a lioness who, with a vehement and irrepressible urge, goes to seek her cubs when they have been taken from her. And so impatient is this love that a man cannot long remain in this state without either gaining the object of his desire or dying.

But I must not fail here to mention the reason why this Divine light does not illumine the soul as soon as it strikes it, but causes at first the darkness and the trials of which we have spoken. To say it once more: The darkness and the other adversities which the soul experiences when this Divine light first strikes it, are not inherent in or caused by this light, but are darknesses and faults of the soul itself; and this light illumines the soul so that it may see them. We may truthfully say, therefore, that this Divine light illumines the soul from the beginning, but at first the soul cannot see [by means of this light] anything beyond that which is around it, or rather, within it—namely, its own darkness and misery. This darkness and misery it now sees through the mercy of God. And once the soul has been purged by the knowledge of these darknesses and miseries in its own being, it is given eyes to see the blessings of this Divine light.

And thus the youth of the soul is restored, and it is clothed with the new man, who, as St. Paul says, is created in the image of God (cf. Eph. 4:24). This, however, is nothing but the illumination of the understanding with supernatural light, so that the human understanding becomes Divine through its union with God. In the same way the will is enkindled with Divine love, so that it now becomes no less than a Divine and divinely loving will, united and made one with the Divine will and love. And so, too, it is with the memory and with the affections and desires: they are all transformed and divinely transfigured, so that even here on earth the soul will be a soul of Heaven, and more Divine than human. And thus the soul has every reason to add the third and fourth lines of the stanza, which read:

"Oh, blessed lot!
I went forth unseen."

CHAPTER XIV

Explanation of the last three lines of the first stanza.

The soul compares itself to a man who, in order to accomplish his task with greater calm, leaves his house in the darkness of the night, when everyone else in the house is at rest, so that no one can disturb him. Thus the soul goes forth from its house, because it intends to perform a deed both heroic and very rare—namely, to become united with its Divine Beloved—and because the Beloved can be found only outside the house and in solitude. The soul in love, in order to attain the goal of its longing, had to go forth at night, when all the lodgers of the house were asleep, that is, when the lower activities, the passions, and the desires of the soul were subdued and at rest. They are the servants of the house, and when they are awake they do not permit the soul to free itself from them and thus hinder it in its pursuit of the blessings of grace. For the natural capacity of the soul is wholly insufficient for the reception of the supernatural goods which God infuses into the soul passively, mysteriously, and in silence. And thus it is necessary that all the faculties should remain passive and not interpose their own base activities and vile inclinations.

It was therefore a "blessed lot" for the soul that in this night God put to sleep all the servants of the house— that is, all the faculties, passions, affections, and desires of the sensual as well as the spiritual part of the soul, so that, "without being observed"—that is, without being hindered by any of these—it could attain to the spiritual union of the perfect love of God. It seems to me, however, that only the soul who has experienced this can understand it; and only then will the soul have learned something about the true liberty and the wealth of the life of the spirit and about the inestimable blessings which derive from it.

CHAPTER XV

*The second stanza: The soul goes forth in disguise
and ascends on the ladder of faith.*

"Secure and protected by darkness,
I climbed the secret ladder, in disguise,
—Oh, blessed lot!—
In darkness, veiled and concealed I went,
Leaving behind my house in deepest rest."

In this stanza the soul sings of some other distinctive properties of this dark night and speaks again of the great blessings that came to it in the wake of this night. The soul wishes to meet the tacit objection that, by exposing itself to the tormenting anxieties, doubts, fears, and terrors of this dark night, it was running the risk of being lost. The soul denies this and says that, on the contrary, it has gained itself in the darkness of this night and has, moreover, escaped very subtly from all those enemies who were previously impeding its every step. For in the darkness of this night the soul changed its garments and disguised itself by putting on a tri-colored vestment, of which we shall have more to say afterwards. I escaped, says the soul, by a concealed ladder, of which no one in the house knew—the ladder of living faith. Thus "veiled and concealed," the soul went forth, in order the better to pursue its goal, and it therefore continues its song with the line:

"Secure and protected by darkness."

CHAPTER XVI

Though in darkness, the soul walks securely.

The sensual and the spiritual desires are now put to sleep and mortified so that they can no longer enjoy the taste of any Divine or human thing; the affections of the soul are restrained and subdued so that they can neither move nor find support in anything; the imagination is bound and can no longer reflect in a rational manner; the memory has lost its strength; the understanding is in darkness, unable to comprehend anything; and hence the will, too, is in aridity and constraint. In short, all the faculties are void and useless; and, in addition to all this, a thick and heavy cloud oppresses the soul and keeps it, as it were, away from God. It is in this kind of darkness that the soul, according to its own words, travels securely. For, when all these operations and movements are arrested, it is evident that the soul is safe from going astray. And the deeper the darkness is in which the soul travels and the more the soul is voided of its natural operations, the greater is its security.

Now if the soul observes itself at the time of this darkness, it will soon notice how safe it is from vainglory, pride, and presumption, from vain and false joy and many other things. And so we see clearly that, by walking in dark faith, the soul by no means runs the risk of being lost, but, on the contrary, is gaining much, since in this state it is perfecting itself in all the virtues.

Therefore, oh spiritual soul, when you find your desire obscured, your affections in aridity and constraint, and your faculties deprived of their capacities for any internal exercise: be not saddened by this, but rather consider it a blessed lot, since God is now about to liberate you from yourself and to take the labor from your hands. For with your own powers, no matter how well you might have used them, you would never have been able to work so efficiently, perfectly, and securely as now, when God takes your hand and guides you in darkness to a goal and by a way which you would never have found with the aid of your own eyes and feet, no matter how sturdy a traveller you may be.

When an explorer wants to travel into new and unknown lands, he must seek new roads of which he does not know anything either by his own past experience or by the reports of others. Similarly, when the soul is making most progress, it is travelling in darkness and unknowing. And since, as we have said, God is the teacher and guide of such a blind soul, it may—once it has learned to understand this —truly and wholeheartedly rejoice and say: I travelled "securely and protected by darkness."

There is yet another reason why the soul has walked securely in this darkness, and this is because its way has been a way of suffering. For the road of suffering is far more secure and profitable than that of rejoicing and of action: first, because in suffering man receives added strength from God, while in action and in any kind of fruition the soul is indulging its own weaknesses and imperfections; and second, because in suffering the soul activates the virtues and thus becomes purer, wiser, and more cautious.

But there is another and even more potent cause of the soul's security on this dark road, and this cause is the dark light or wisdom of God. For this dark night of contemplation so strongly attracts and envelops the soul, and brings it so near to God, that He Himself now protects it and detaches it from all that is not God. And since the soul is now, as it were, undergoing a cure, so that it may regain its health (that is, God, Who is the health of the soul), His Majesty restricts it to a diet and an abstinence from all things, so that it may lose its appetite for all of them. The soul is like a sick man who is carefully nursed in his house; he is being protected from the wind, from the rays of the sun, and from noise; and he is given only small portions of delicate food—food that is more nourishing than pleasing to the palate.

Finally, there is one more reason, no less weighty than those mentioned, which makes it clear to our understanding why the soul walks securely in this darkness. We are referring to the fortitude which is transmitted to the soul by the influx of these dark and turbulent waters of God. For the soul forthwith perceives in itself a firm determination and resolve to do nothing that it knows will offend God, and to omit nothing that it knows will serve and please Him. All the desires, energies, and faculties of the soul are now detached from all other things, and all its powers are recollected and employed in the effort to please Him. In this manner the soul goes forth from itself and from all created things and travels "securely and protected by darkness" toward the sweet and blissful union of love with God.

CHAPTER XVII

This dark contemplation is a secret, nameless, purely spiritual wisdom.

"I climbed the secret ladder, in disguise."

In order to understand the three specific terms which occur in this line, it is necessary to explain three things. Two of these terms—namely, "secret" and "ladder"—are used with reference to the dark night of contemplation, while the third expression—namely, "in disguise"—refers to the way the soul conducts itself in this night.

First of all, the soul calls this dark contemplation "secret," because, as we have indicated above, it is that mystical theology which the theologians describe as secret or hidden wisdom, and which, according to St. Thomas [Aquinas], is communicated and infused into the soul

through love (cf. *Summa Theologica,* 2a, 2ae, q. 45, a.2).
This is being done secretly, while the natural activity of the
understanding and of the other faculties is in darkness. And,
inasmuch as this contemplation is not brought about by any
of these faculties, but is infused by the Holy Spirit, without
the soul's knowledge or understanding, it is called secret.

It is not however, for this reason alone that this contemplation may be called secret, but also because of the
effects which it produces in the soul. For this contemplation
is secret or hidden not only in the darknesses and afflictions
of purgation, but likewise afterwards in illumination, when
this wisdom is communicated to the soul with much greater
clarity. Even then, however, it is still so secret that the
soul is unable to name it or to speak of it. Not only has
the soul no desire to speak of it or to name it, but it is
unable to find any suitable similitude by which it might
describe such a sublime knowledge and such a delicate
spiritual experience. For this inward wisdom is so simple,
general, and spiritual that it cannot enter into the understanding in any conceptual form or sensory image, notwithstanding the fact that the soul is clearly aware that it is
partaking of that wondrous and blissful wisdom. For it is a
characteristic of the language of God that, on account of
its being so intimate and spiritual, it wholly transcends the
sphere of sense and at once nullifies and voids all the
harmony and capacity of the internal and external senses.
And, inasmuch as the wisdom of this contemplation is the
language of God addressed to the soul, and spoken by pure
spirit to pure spirit, nothing that is less than spirit can
comprehend it, and it therefore remains hidden to the senses.

This mystical wisdom is called "secret" also on account
of the fact that it has the property of hiding the soul within
itself. For it sometimes takes possession of the soul and
draws it into its secret abyss, in such a way that the soul
clearly sees what a distance there is between it and every
creature and how far it has been carried away. It feels as
though it had been placed into a profound and vast solitude,

into an immense and boundless desert, inaccessible to any human being. And the deeper, vaster, and more hidden the solitude, the more it delights and pleases the soul. This abyss of wisdom greatly exalts and enriches the soul and places it at the very source of the science of love.

This property of secrecy or concealment and of transcendence with respect to the natural capacity pertains to this Divine contemplation not only because it is supernatural, but also because it acts as a guide in leading the soul to the perfections of the union with God. And inasmuch as these perfections cannot be known in the human manner, they must be approached by human unknowing and by supernatural ignorance. For, speaking mystically (as we are doing here), these Divine things and perfections are not known and understood in their true being when they are merely sought or theoretically explored, but only when they have been found and practically experienced.

CHAPTER XVIII

This secret wisdom is a ladder on which the soul climbs upward and downward, until it attains to mystical union.

It remains now to consider the second point, namely, to explain in what sense this secret wisdom is also a "ladder." This name applies, first of all, because, just as soldiers climb up on ladders and enter fortified places in order to gain possession of provisions, material treasures, and other objects, so the soul, by means of this secret contemplation, mounts (without knowing how) to gain knowledge and possession of the goods and treasures of Heaven.

Furthermore, we may call this secret contemplation a ladder because, even as the steps of a ladder serve men to ascend and descend, so this secret contemplation—by means of the identical supernatural communications—alternately raises the soul up to God and humbles it with respect to its own self. For it is the common property of all truly Divine communications that they both humble and exalt the soul. For on this road every descent is an ascent, and every ascent is a descent, because "everyone who humbles himself shall be exalted, and he who exalts himself shall be humbled" (Luke 14:11). And it is the ordinary way and rule of the state of contemplation that one never remains for long at the same place, but is continually ascending and descending, until the soul arrives at the state of quiet. For, since the state of perfection consists in the perfect love of God and the contempt of oneself, the soul cannot be without this dichotomy, namely, the knowledge of God and the knowledge of its own self—that is, without ever recurring exaltations and humiliations—until it has acquired the habits of perfection. Only then will this ascending and descending cease, because the soul will then have reached its goal and will have become united with Him Who stands at the summit of this ladder and upon Whom the ladder leans and rests.

This ladder of contemplation is prefigured in that ladder which Jacob saw in his dream, on which angels were ascending from man to God and descending from God to man (cf. Gen. 28:12). And all this, according to Holy Scripture, took place by night, when Jacob was asleep, which indicates how secret and how different from the human mode of knowing is this road and this ascent to God.

But the principal characteristic and the main reason why this contemplation is here called a "ladder" is that it is a *science of love,* that is, an infused and loving knowledge of God, which at one and the same time illumines the soul and enkindles it with love, to the end that it may be raised step by step to God its Creator. For it is love alone that unites and joins the soul with God. And in order that this may be seen more clearly, we shall here indicate the several steps of this Divine ladder and point out briefly the marks and effects of each, so that the soul may be able to observe on which of them it is standing. We shall therefore now proceed to distinguish these steps by their effects, as do St. Bernard [of Clairvaux] and St. Thomas [Aquinas].

CHAPTER XIX

Explanation of the ten steps of this mystical ladder, according to St. Bernard and St. Thomas.

There are, as we have said, ten steps on this ladder of love, by which the soul ascends, one by one, to God. The *first step* of love causes the soul to become sick, and this is for its own good. On this step stood the Bride [in the Song of Solomon] when she said: "I adjure you, daughters of Jerusalem, if you find my Beloved, tell Him that I am sick with love" (Canticles 5:8). This sickness, however, is not unto death, but for the glory of God; for in this sickness the soul dies only to sin and to all things that are not God. And the soul does not fall into this sickness unless an excess of love is communicated to it. And now it can no longer find any pleasure, support, consolation, and rest in anything. It therefore begins at once to climb to the second step.

The *second step* causes the soul to seek God without ceasing. And thus, when the Bride says that she sought her Beloved as she was lying upon her bed, and found Him not, she immediately adds: "I will rise and seek Him Whom my soul loves" (Cant. 3:2). On this step the soul is so filled to overflowing with love that it seeks the Beloved in all things, and in all its thoughts it has in mind the Beloved. When it eats, when it sleeps, in its night-watches, and in whatever else it does, all its care is for the Beloved. And now, as love gradually recovers its health and is gaining new strength on this second step, it begins at once to climb to the third, by means of a new purgation in this dark night.

The *third step* of the ladder of love activates the soul and fills it with a burning zeal to work without wearying.

On this step the valiant deeds which the soul may have done for its Beloved appear to it as very small, and the long hours which it may have spent in serving Him appear as very short. The soul considers itself quite useless in all that it does, and thinks that it is wasting its life in idleness. And from this springs another admirable effect, namely, the firm conviction that it is far worse than all other souls: first and foremost, because love makes it realize more and more how much it owes to God; and second, because it recognizes how faulty and imperfect are the many works which it does for God in this state. And this anxious care, together with many similar effects that are produced in the soul on this third step of love, impart to it the courage and strength to mount to the fourth step.

The *fourth step* of this ladder of love produces in the soul a continuous suffering for the sake of the Beloved, but a suffering which the soul endures without wearying. For, as St. Augustine says, love makes all things that are burdensome and painful so easy that they appear as nothing. In this state the spirit gains so much strength that is is capable of keeping the flesh in complete subjection and is as little encumbered by it as a tree is by one of its leaves.

Exceedingly lofty, then, is this fourth step of love; for, as the soul in this state goes ever after God with truest love and with the spiritual resolve to suffer for His sake, His Majesty frequently grants it the sweet joys of a visitation in the spirit; for the boundless love of Christ, the Word, cannot allow the loving soul to suffer without coming to its aid. This He affirmed through the mouth of Jeremiah, where we read: "I have remembered you, and have pitied your tender youth, when you went after Me through desert land" (Jer. 2:2). This fourth step, then, enkindles the soul and makes it burn with such desire for God that it causes it to rise to the fifth step.

The *fifth step* of this ladder of love causes in the soul an impatient striving and yearning for God. On this step the longing of the loving soul for the possession of the Beloved and for union with Him has become so vehement that every delay, however brief it be, appears to the soul very long, wearisome, and oppressive, since its only thought is how to find the Beloved. On this step the lover must either behold the Beloved, or die. The soul is thus languishing with hunger, and its only nourishment is love; and hence it rises to the sixth step.

CHAPTER XX

The five remaining steps of love. The tenth step: the beatific vision.

The *sixth step* causes the soul to run swiftly to meet God and to experience His nearness in many palpable touches. Its hope runs after Him without wearying; for hope has been made strong by love, so that it may fly swiftly. And the cause of this swiftness is that the soul's love is greatly enlarged on this step, and its purification is almost complete; and thus the soul at once advances to the seventh step.

The *seventh step* of this ladder makes the soul very daring. Here love is no longer guided by prudent judgment or daunted in its hope, nor does it accept any counsel to draw back. For the grace which God here grants the soul causes it to become very determined in its boldness. By this attitude it confirms what the Apostle says, namely, that love believes all things, hopes all things, and is capable of doing and enduring all things (cf. 1 Cor. 13:7). On this step the Bride grew bold, and said: "I thirst for a kiss from these lips" (Cant. 1:1). To this the soul could never dare to aspire unless it had first received the inward grace bestowed upon it "by the sceptre of the King"; for otherwise it would fall from the other steps which it has mounted and to which it must cling with humility. From the daring and freedom which God grants to the soul on this seventh step follows the eighth, on which the soul is united with the Beloved.

The *eighth step* of love, then, causes the soul to seize the Beloved and hold Him fast without letting Him go, according to the words of the Bride: "I found Him Whom my heart and soul love; and now that He is mine I will never let Him go" (Cant. 3:4). On this step of union the longing of the soul is satisfied, but not continuously; for some souls gain a temporary foothold on this step and then lose it again. If it were otherwise and this union were to continue, they would in fact attain to a certain state of glory in this life.

The *ninth step* of love causes the soul to burn with sweet rapture. This is the state of perfection, that is, the state of those perfect souls who are aflame with the sweet love of God. This blissful flame of love is caused by the Holy Ghost, by virtue of the union which these souls have with God. And there are no words with which the abundant graces and treasures of God which the soul enjoys on this step can be described.

The *tenth and last step* of this secret ladder of love causes the soul to become wholly assimilated to God, by virtue of the *clear vision of God* to which the soul that has ascended to the ninth step in this life, attains immediately after it has gone forth from the flesh. For these souls, who are few, enter not into purgatory, since they have already been wholly purged by love. Of these souls St. Matthew speaks when he says: "Blessed are the pure of heart; they shall see God" (Matt. 5:8). And this vision is the cause of the perfect likeness of the soul to God, for, according to the words of St. John, "we know that we shall be like Him" (1 John 3:2). Not because the soul will have the capacity of God, for this is impossible; but because all that the soul is will be like to God, so that the soul will be *God by participation*.

On this last step of pure vision, which is also the last step on this ladder, nothing is any longer hidden from the soul, because it has now been wholly assimilated to God. In this manner, then, the soul—by this mystical Divine

Wisdom and this mystical love—rises above all things and above itself, and ascends to God.

CHAPTER XXI

The meaning of the word "disguise" and the colors of the soul's disguise.

Now that we have explained the reason why the soul calls this contemplation a "secret ladder," it remains for us to explain the meaning of the expression "in disguise," and to state why the soul says that it went forth by this secret ladder "in disguise."

"To disguise oneself" means to hide and cover oneself beneath another person's garment and figure—sometimes in order to express externally one's love and affection for someone dear to one's heart, and thereby to gain this person's favor and good will; sometimes, again, in order to hide oneself from one's adversaries, so that one may the better accomplish one's purpose. And at such times one chooses a shape and color of dress which best indicate and express the sentiments of the heart and which best serve to conceal one from one's enemies.

The soul, then, which is in this state is enkindled with love for Christ, its Spouse, Whose grace and goodwill it longs and desires to gain; it goes forth attired in a disguise which most vividly makes manifest the affections of its spirit and which will most safely protect it on its journey from its adversaries and enemies, which are the devil, the world, and the flesh. For this reason the attire which the soul wears is of three principal colors—white, green, and red. These three colors signify the three theological virtues —*faith, hope,* and *love.* By these virtues the soul will not only gain the grace and goodwill of its Beloved, but it will travel completely protected and perfectly safe from its three enemies. For *faith* is a white tunic of such splendor that it dazzles the eyes of all human understanding. And thus, when the soul travels clad in the vestment of faith, the devil can neither see it nor harm it.

Over this white tunic of faith the soul now puts on the second color, namely a green vestment, which signifies the virtue of *hope*. By this virtue the soul is delivered and protected from the second enemy, which is the world. For this verdant color of living hope in God gives the soul such vital strength and courage in its aspiration to the blessings of eternal life that, by comparison with the objects of hope, all the things of this world appear—as indeed they are— dry, barren, lifeless, and worthless. The soul here divests and strips itself of all these worldly vestments and garments and henceforth lives clothed only in the hope of eternal life. And, clad in this garment of hope, the soul is so pleasing to its Beloved that one may truly say that it obtains from Him as much as it hopes for.

Over these white and green vestments—as the crowning perfection of this whole new attire—the soul now puts on the third color, which is a splendid toga of deep red and which signifies *love,* the third theological virtue. This garment of self-giving love protects and hides the soul from its third enemy, which is the flesh. For where there is true love of God, there is no longer any place for either love of self or love of anything that pertains to the self. This love, moreover, strengthens the other virtues, imparting to them vigor and power to protect the soul, and imbuing them with grace and beauty to please the Beloved with them; for without holy love no virtue is pleasing to God.

Since it is, then, the function of these three virtues to separate and detach the soul from all that is less than God, they consequently serve to bring about the ultimate union of the soul with God. And thus it is impossible for the soul to attain to this perfect union with God through love, unless it travels in truth clad in the vestments of these three virtues. To have succeeded in clothing itself in such attire and in wearing it until it will have attained the end of its desire and striving—the union of love—is thus indeed a great good fortune or a "blessed lot" for the soul.

CHAPTERS XXII AND XXIII

Explanation of line four of the second stanza.

The most important object of my task, the one which chiefly led me to undertake it, is almost attained. As I pointed out in the Prologue, the main purpose I had in mind was to explain this night to many souls who pass through it and yet know very little about it.

The reason why the soul considers its passing through the dark night a "blessed lot" is given in the following line:

"In darkness, veiled and concealed I went."

The word "concealed" means as much as "in a secret hiding-place." And when the soul says that it went forth "in darkness, veiled and concealed," it is trying to describe as clearly as possible the great security which it has gained by means of this dark contemplation. Furthermore, when the soul says "in darkness, veiled and concealed," it means that, because it thus travelled in darkness, it was hidden and concealed from the wiles and snares of the devil. And it is in this total darkness and in concealment from the enemy that the soul receives the spiritual graces of God. The reason for this is that His Majesty dwells substantially in the soul, in a place to which neither angel nor demon has access. And neither angel nor demon can attain to an understanding of what comes to pass in this secret hiding-place and of the secret communications between the soul and God. For, inasmuch as these communications and spiritual graces are worked by God Himself, they are wholly Divine and are in their sublimity substantial manifestations of the supernatural union between the soul and God. And, since these touches represent the highest degree of *mystical prayer,* the soul here receives more graces and blessings than in all other forms of prayer taken together.

When these graces are granted to the soul "in concealment," that is, in the spirit alone, the soul sees itself set apart and separated from its sensual and inferior part to such a degree that it clearly recognizes in itself two distinct parts and comes to believe that the one is very remote and wholly divorced from the other. And in a certain sense this is actually so, since the operations of the soul are now purely spiritual and the sensual part receives no longer any communication. And in this concealment of unitive contemplation the spiritual desires and passions of the soul are almost completely appeased and calmed. And thus, speaking of its higher part, the soul says in the last line of the second stanza that its house was now "in deepest rest."

CHAPTER XXIV

Conclusion of the explanation of the second stanza.

"Leaving behind my house in deepest rest."

With these words the soul wants to convey the following meaning: Since both my higher and my lower part were at last at rest with respect to the desires and faculties, I went forth to the supernatural union of love with God. And because in the combat of this dark night the soul was assailed and purged in a twofold manner—namely, in its sensual and spiritual part, so likewise it attains to peace and rest in a twofold manner, that is, in its sensual and spiritual part. For this reason the soul *twice* pronounces *the same words*—namely, in this and in the preceding stanza. And in order that these two parts of the soul may be raised to the Divine union of love, they must first be transformed, ordered, and tranquillized with respect to sense and spirit, in accordance with the state of innocence that was enjoyed by Adam. And thus this line which, in the first stanza, referred to the tranquillity of the lower and sensual part, is used, in the second stanza, with particular reference to the higher and spiritual part.

This tranquillity and peace of the spiritual house becomes an habitual and perfect property of the soul (in so far as this is possible according to the conditions of this life), by means of those substantial touches of Divine union of which we have just spoken. This union is the *Divine betrothal* between the soul and the Son of God. And as soon as these two houses of the soul with all their lodgers—namely, the faculties and desires—have been wholly appeased, silenced and made strong in the calm of this night, Divine Wisdom immediately unites itself with the soul by a new bond of loving possession, so that there shall be fulfilled what is written in the Book of Wisdom: "There was deep silence all around, and night had but finished half of her journey, when from Thy royal throne, oh Lord, leaped down Thy omnipotent word" (Wisd. 18:14).

CHAPTER XXV

The third stanza.

Oh, blissful night!
Oh, secret night, when I remained unseeing and unseen,
When the flame burning in my heart
Was my only light and guide.

In continuing the explanation of its spiritual night, the soul makes use once more of the metaphor and simile of temporal night. It praises and extols the excellent qualities which it has found and used on its journey through this night and which are to aid it in the speedy and secure attainment of its desired goal. And it mentions specifically three of these qualities.

The *first* is that in this blissful night God blesses the soul with a contemplation so solitary and hidden, and so remote and estranged from sense, that neither the things of the sensual sphere nor any creature can touch it so as to disturb it and detain it on the road of the union of love.

The *second* quality is an effect of the spiritual darkness of this night, wherein all the faculties of the higher part of the soul are immersed in darkness. And since the soul neither sees nor is able to perceive anything or to tarry in anything that is not God, it gives itself wholly to God.

The *third* quality has its cause in the fact that the soul no longer leans on any particular inward illumination of the understanding nor on any external guide, to receive consolation and support on this lofty road; for the black darkness of this night has deprived it of all this. It is now moved and guided by love alone, whose flame burns in its heart and makes it yearn for the Beloved. And thus on the road of solitude it soars upward to God.

[The (incomplete) text of "The Dark Night of the Soul" ends with the repetition of the first line of the third stanza. Six of the eight stanzas of the poem remain thus without a commentary. This loss is, however, in part made up by the commentary that accompanies the "Spiritual Canticle," another one of the great mystical works of St. John of the Cross].